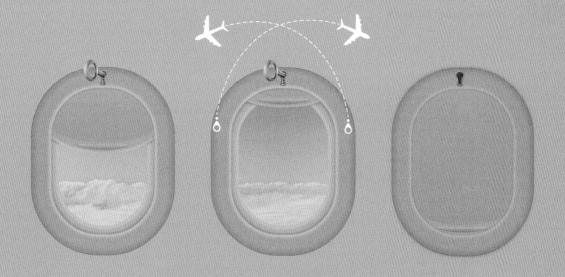

외항사 면접관이 알려주는 단기 합격을 위한 **완벽 가이드**

항공 영어 인터뷰
Airline English Interview

사람은 누구나 꿈이 있습니다.

꿈은 막연하게 동경하는 것이 아니라 이루기 위해 작은 것부터 하나씩 노력해야 실제로 이루어질 수 있고, 또 반드시 이루어집니다. 만약 여러분이 승무원이 되고자 한다면 승무원의 태도, 승무원의 마음가짐으로 자신을 이미지 메이킹 해야 합니다. 평상 시 태도, 타인을 향한 배려, 스마일 등 면접 연습을 하기 전 '나'를 바꾸는 작업부터 해야 하는 것입니다. 가령 앉는 자세가 구부정하고 단정치 못했다면 지금부터 예쁘게 바르게 앉는 연습부터 해보는 것이죠. 처음은 힘들겠지만 익숙해지면 자연스러워 질 것입니다. 이것은 그대로 면접에도 영향을 미친다는 것을 명심 해야만 합니다.

두번째로 타인을 향한 배려가 몸에 배어 있어야 합니다. 이를 위해서 제일 필요한 것이 바로 '공감능력'입니다. 나 자신이 완전히 상대방이 되어서 생각할 수 있어야 합니다. 즉, '입장 바꿔 생각하는' 연습을 평상시 생활속에서 꾸준히 하며 항공사 면접 시 도움이 될 수 있도록 해보아야 합니다. 꾸준한 작은 노력으로 이는 분명 습관이 될 수 있으며 또 성공적인 면접으로 이끌 것입니다. 특히 다국적 승무원과 함께 일하는 외국항공사일수록 고객입장에서 생각할 줄 알고 다른 동료입장에서도 생각할 줄 아는 훌륭한 공감능력을 가진 지원자를 선발하려 한다는 점을 기억하시기 바랍니다. 이 교재는 외항사 채용에 있어서 2018년부터 새롭게 바뀐 면접절차와 내용 그리고 기출문제들을 담아 더 쉽게 면접에 임할 수 있도록 기획하였습니다. 채용 시 어느정도 변동되기도 하나, 현재 진행되고 있는 면접 절차와 기출을 충분히 파악하고 있다면 큰 틀은 바뀌지 않을 것입니다. 어떠한 상황에서도 당황하지 않고 바른 자세, 밝은 표정, 매너를 갖출 수 있도록 하고, 순발력과 긍정적 마인드를 갖추고 있다면 어떠한 질문을 받아도 막힘이 없을 것이라 생각합니다.

꾸준히 노력하며 포기하지 않는 한 여러분의 꿈은 반드시 이루어질 것입니다. 건투를 빕니다.

이혜진

Epilogue

이 교재는 국내 항공사 영어면접을 비롯해서 외국 항공사 1차부터 최종 면접까지 대비할 수 있게 구성하였다.

먼저 오리엔테이션 부분에서 면접의 형태 및 주안점, 영어 면접에서 제일 기본적으로 높게 평가되는 '태도'에 대해서 집중적으로 소개하였다.

국내 항공사의 경우 기존의 면접 실무 교재에서 다루는 면접 복장, 메이크업, 사진 등은 생략하였고, 외국 항공사 지원 시 필요한 정보, 즉 면접 복장, 메이크업, 사진 등의 정보를 담았다. 또한 면접 시 중요한 태도 및 주안점을 기술하였기 때문에 실제 면접 준비 시 도움이 될거라 생각한다.

중요한 파트이기 때문에 이 부분을 기본으로 숙지하고 그 다음 Chapter 1로 들어가 실제 면접 대비 답변 연습을 하기 바란다. Chapter마다 각각의 주제를 가지고 다양한 영어 면접 질문에 대비할 수 있도록 하였다. 기본이 되는 Personal Data 비롯 Small talk 부분은 국내 항공사 영어 면접 및 외국 항공사 1차부터 최종까지 모든 영어 면접의 시작 시 반드시 나오는 부분이므로 쉬운 답변이라도 어떻게 면접관에게 답변할지 충분한 연습을 하기 바란다. 가령 '인사'의 경우 반 자동적으로 먼저 면접관에게 인사할 수 있도록 인사말을 익혀야 하며 쉬운 답변일수록 의외로 준비가 부족하여 짧은 시간 말이 나오지 않는 경우가 있으므로 많은 연습을 요한다. Small talk 부분에서 그 날 면접의 당락이 좌우된다 해도 과언이 아니다. 실제로 면접자의 성격이 드러나는 부분이므로 면접관은 간단한 인사에도 크게 평가를 하기 때문이다. 외국 항공사 스크리닝 면접의 경우 Small talk만으로 당락을 가르는 이유가 여기에 있다고 하겠다.

면접 준비가 완료되면 이제 주제별로 영어 면접 대비를 하여 나만의 답변 셋팅이 이루어져야 한다. 국내 항공사 영어 면접의 경우 거의 기출문제에서 나오기 때문에 답변 준비가 철저하면 쉽게 영어 면접을 볼 수가 있으나 외국 항공사는 그렇지가 않다. 대부분이 'Have you~?'로 시작되는 질문, 즉 경험을 묻는 질문이기 때문에 나만의 스토리텔링이 필요하다. 그 경험담 속에 나의 긍정적인 태도, 팀웍, 서비스 마인드 등이 보여져야 하므로 제일 먼저 철저히 답변을 세팅해 보는게 중요하다 하겠다. 사람마다 경험이 틀리기 때문에 교재에 나오는 경험이 내 경험과 같을 순 없지만 이 교재에서 보여지는 예시 답변을 통해 힌트를 얻을 수 있을 것이라 생각한다. 영어 실력을 단기간에 늘릴 수 있는 유일한 방법은 다양한 표현을 외우고 실제 사용해야 한다. 그러므로 여러분의 답변이 준비가 된 후 스터디를 통해 모의 면접의 시간을 자주 가지며 답변을 사용하는 기회를 가진다면 자연스레 기본적인 영어실력까지 향상될거라 생각한다.

이는 또한 필기시험 중 에세이 문제에 대비할 수 있는 초석이 될 것이다.

대부분의 에세이 주제는 실제 면접에서 물어보는 질문들이기 때문이다.

예시 답변 구성은 짧게는 국내 항공사용부터 필요 시 길게는 외국 항공사용으로 나누었다.

모든 질문은 따로 언급이 없는 한 국내/외국 항공사에서 공통으로 나올 수 있는 문제들이고 각각의 Chapter 안에서 외국 항공사에서 더 나올 수 있는 문제들은 따로 표시해서 다루었으니 참고하길 바란다.

예시 답변이 나의 경우와 비슷하다면 약간을 수정해 나만의 답변을 만들도록 하고 그렇지 않더라도 다양한 표현의 예시문이 여러분의 답변을 준비하는데 충분한 참고 자료가 될 것이라고 믿는다.

나의 답변을 만들어 노트에 직접 질문과 답변을 적어서 차후 면접 시 한 번씩 보며 모의 면접을 하고 간다면 자신감도 생길 것이다.

Contents

Chapter 1 ː Orientation ㆍ 2

Chapter 2 ː Key Points,
Tips and Guidelines for Interview ㆍ 46

Chapter 3   **English Interview** · 62

항공 영어 인터뷰
Airline English Interview

Contents

항공 영어 인터뷰

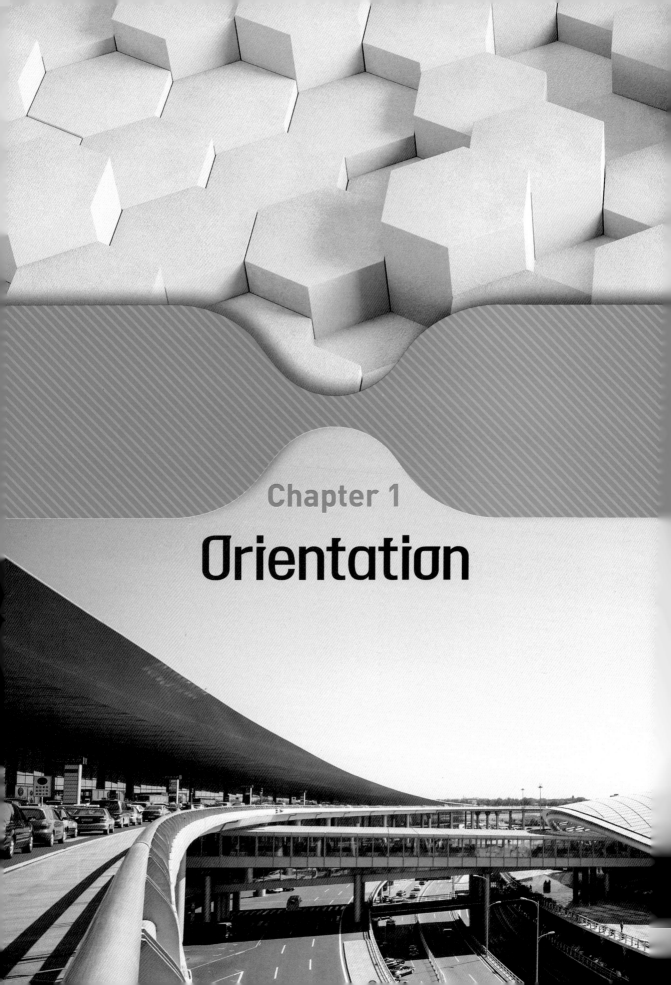

Chapter 1
Orientation

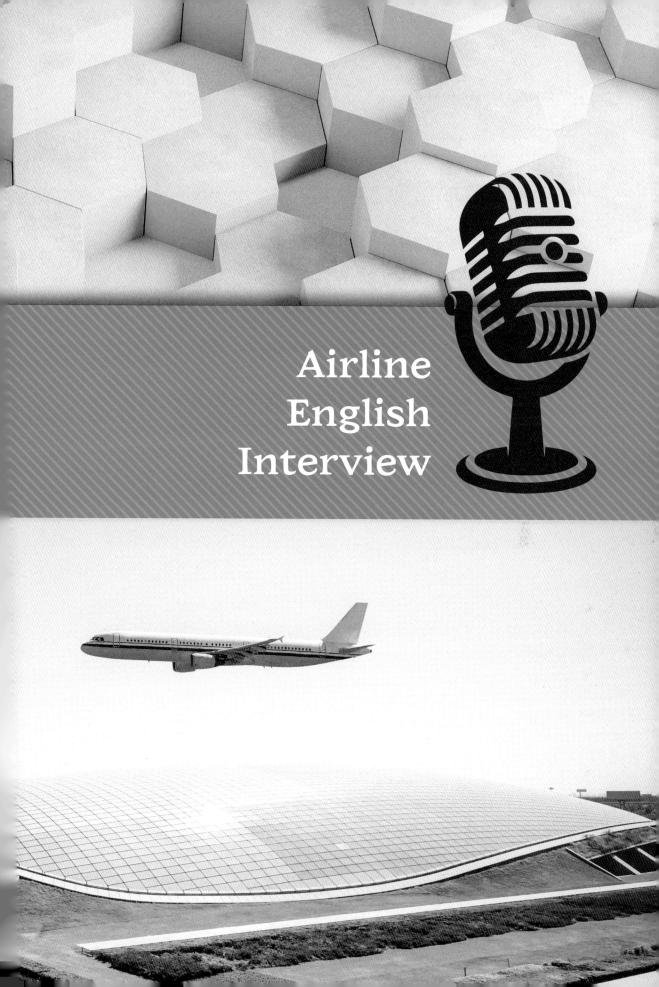

Airline
English
Interview

외국 항공사 소개
(현재 한국에서 활발히 채용하고 있는 항공사)

1 에미레이트 항공(Emirates Airlines)

 객실 승무원

에미레이트는 1985년 10월 25일, Boeing 737과 Airbus 300 B4 단 두 대의 임대 항공기로 두바이에서 첫 운항을 시작했다. 에미레이트는 이제 물량이 아니라 품질에 목표를 두고, 근거리 지역의 여행 서비스를 제공하던 초기 단계를 지나, 비즈니스의 모든 측면에서 최고 수준의 품질을 보장하는 것으로 유명한 세계 일류의 여행 및 관광 그룹으로 성장했다. 가장 최신 기종의 항공기로 전 세계 140개 이상의 도시를 취항하고 있는 에미레이트는 정기적인 항공기 업그레이드를 통해 승객들에게 최고 수준의 탑승 경험을 지속적으로 제공한다. 항공기 종류로는 A380, A330-900, A350-900, B777-200LR, B777-300ER, B777-8X, 777-9X , B787-10 이 있다.

에미레이트는 두바이 정부가 전적으로 소유하고 있는 국영 기업이지만, 자국 기업 보호를 통해서가 아니라, 두바이 정부의 영공 개방 정책에 따라 지속적으로 증가하는 많은 국제 항공사와의 치열한 경쟁을 통해 발전을 거듭하고 있다. 에미레이트는

출처 : Emirates 홈페이지

이러한 정책을 지지할 뿐만 아니라, 이 정책이 에미레이트의 위상과 경쟁력을 유지하는 데 필수적이라고 생각한다. 두바이 정부는 초기 투자 이후 에미레이트를 완전한 독립 기업으로 간주하고 있으며, 이에 따라 에미레이트는 건실하게 성장하고 있다. 매년 20% 이상의 성장률을 유지하고 있으며, 설립 3년째부터 매년 흑자를 기록하고 있다.

이렇듯 에미레이트는 폭발적인 성장을 계속하면서도 업계 최상의 서비스를 제공하기 위해 끊임없이 노력하고 있다. 또한 에미레이트 항공은 수년 간 품질 높은 기내식, 다양한 기내 엔터테인먼트, 전반적인 고품격 서비스를 제공하는 항공사로 인정받고 있으며, 올해의 항공사(Aviation Business Awards), 세계 최우수 엔터테인먼트 제공 항공사(World Airline Entertainment Association), 최우수 국제항공사 등 다양한 수상경력을 자랑하고 있다. 에미레이트는 마일리지 프로그램 Skywards(블루, 실버, 그리고 골드 세 가지 회원 등급으로 나뉘어짐)을 제공하며 여행보상 서비스를 실시하고 있다.

• **국 명**	아랍에미리트 연합국(영어 : The United Arab Emirates, 아랍어 : Al Imarat Al Arabiyan Al Muttahida)
• **수 도**	아부다비(Abu Dhabi)
• **면 적**	83,600km^2

• **기 후**	아열대 소한기후
• **평균기온**	4월–10월 38–47℃, 11월–3월 10–35℃
• **강수량**	연평균 42mm
• **주요자원**	원유, 가스
• **원유**	매장량 981억배럴(세계 3위), 생산량 200만 배럴/일(99.4. OPEC 쿼타 기준)
• **가스**	매장량 204조 Cubicfeet(세계 4위)
• **민족**	아랍족
• **언어**	아랍어(영어 통용)
• **종교**	이슬람교(수니파 80%, 시아파 20%)
• **정부형태**	7개 에미리트로 형성된 연방, 대통령 중심제
• **독립일**	1971. 12. 2.
• **국경일**	12. 2(연방정부수립일)
• **국경일**	UAE Dirham(AED), 1DH = 100Fils , US$ 1 = DH 3.67

- **두바이(Dubai)**
  - 인구 : 78만명("98년)
  - GCC 지역의 경제·통상활동 중심지로 부상 중
  - 날씨는 여름철(약 45~50도, 고온 건조)을 제외하면 서늘하며 밤엔 쌀쌀함. 집 밖에선 늘 택시로 이동(기본료 약 1,000원)하며 실내는 어디에나 에어콘 시설이 되어 있고 건조해서 습한 우리나라만큼 덥다고 생각되지 않음. 아랍인은 약 10%이며, 백인(유럽쪽)이 많음. 공용어로 영어 이용. 서양에 온 만큼이나 백인 문화가 퍼져있고 규제나 통제를 거의 느끼지 못함. 복장의 제약도 없다.

• **소속**	Emirates Group
• **설립일**	1985년 5월 25일
• **허브공항**	두바이 국제공항(ONLY BASE)
• **동맹**	Skywards
• **대한민국 취항일**	2005년 5월 1일(대한항공 공동 운항)
• **IATA**	EK
• **ICAO**	UAE
• **Slogan**	Fly Better

- **Provider**　　over 20,000 employees across five continents

- **보유항공기종**
  - 총 246대의 항공기 보유
  - A350-900 : 30대
  - A350-900 : 30대
  - B777-300ER :145대
  - 777-9X : 115대
  - A380 : 109대
  - A330-900 : 40대
  - B777-200LR : 10대
  - B777-8X : 3대
  - B787-10 : 40대

- **80여개국 140개 이상 취항 중**

Emirates cabin crew must deliver exceptional customer service experience on every flight. Thus, in addition to the Emirates Cabin Crew requirements above, you should demonstrate:

- A positive attitude and empathy for others
- Strong cultural awareness and the ability to adapt to new environments and people
- Flexibility and the motivation to manage a demanding work schedule
- Qualities necessary to live up to the mission and values that Emirates holds in high regard-Professional, Empathetic, Progressive, Visionary, Cosmopolitan

자격조건	• 고등학교 졸업 이상 • 조인하는 시점 기준으로 만 21세 이상 • 암리치(발꿈치 들고) 212cm 가능한 자 • 영어 구사능력 뛰어난 자. 서비스 경험자 우대 • 해외여행에 결격사유가 없는 자 • 눈에 보이는 상처나 문신이 없어야 함(화장품이나 밴드로 가리는 것 금지) • 신체 건강한 자
채용절차	• 1차 : CV Drop(오픈데이) / 온라인 접수(어세스먼트 데이) • 2차 : 그룹 면접(2회) • 3차 : 1:1 화상면접 *자세한 면접 절차 및 기출문제는 뒤에 다시 다룸
베이스	• 두바이
복리후생	• 주택 지원, 통근 지원, 의료지원, 생명보험, 항공권 지원, 연 30일의 휴가

 지상직 승무원

출처 : Emirates 홈페이지

채용분야	• 여객운송(체크인 카운터), 여객영업(예약발권), 마하바 서비스, 크루즈 서비스
근무지역	• UAE 두바이 국제공항
근무형태	• 스케줄 근무, 주 42시간
복리후생	• 주택 지원, 차량 지원, 각종 보험, 수당, 의료지원, 항공권 지원, 연장 계약(정년 65세)
자격요건	• 나이 : 제한 없음 • 성별 : 제한 없음 • 학력 : 고졸 이상 • 필수 : 영어 가능자, 해외 체류 가능자 • 우대 : 서비스 계통의 근무 경험자, 항공사 또는 여행사 근무 경험자, CRS 자격증, DCS 자격증 소지자, 호텔 및 의료서비스 경험자, 제2외국어 구사자 • 기타 : 항공서비스 업무에 적합한 신체건강에 이상이 없는 자
채용절차	• 서류 전형 → 1차 면접 → 스크리닝 면접 → 최종 면접

2 카타르 항공(Qatar Airways)

객실 승무원

　카타르 항공사는 항공 서비스 평가 기관인 스카이트랙스(Skytrax)로부터 최고 서비스 및 우수성을 인정받아 왔으며 전 세계 6개의 5 Star(Cathay pacific, Singapore Airlines, King Fisher, Malaysia Airlines, Asiana Airlines) 항공사 중 하나로 평가받고 있다.

　카타르 항공사는 가장 혁신적인 항공사 중 하나로 2006년에는 세계 최초로 도하 국제공항에 퍼스트 및 비즈니스 승객들을 위한 프리미엄 터미널을 오픈하였다. 또한 중동 미래 산업의 허브인 도하 신 국제공항(New Doha International Airport)은 2015년 완공될 예정이며 카타르 항공사는 신 공항 개항과 함께 미래 항공업계를 이끌어 나갈 것으로 기대하고 있다.

출처 : Qatar Airways 인스타그램

카타르 항공은 지난 1997년 운항을 시작한 이래 2008년 현재 중동 및 아프리카의 8개국, 아시아 10개국, 유럽 10개국, 북아메리아의 미국을 포함한 80여개의 노선을 확보하고 있다. 2006년 도하 아시안게임을 거점으로 'Your 5 Star Airline' 이라는 문구와 함께 세계적으로 그 영역을 확대하고 있으며, 세계 최고 성장률이라는 수식어에 맞게 지속적으로 노선카타르 항공은 2013년 110대 항공기 보유를 목표로 2007년에는 80대의 Airbus A350, 60대의 Boeing B787, 32대의 Boeing B777을 주문하였으며 나아가 차세대 기종인 최신형 A380을 2010년까지 운행을 목표로 5대 주문하며 전 세계 여러 지역을 빠르게 연결하고 있다.

① 카타르 항공의 마일리지 프로그램(Frequent Flyer Program)

• **Privilege Club** : 카타르 항공의 마일리지 프로그램의 멤버들은 다양한 혜택과 특권을 누릴 수 있다. 티켓을 예약하는 순간부터 최종 목적지 도착까지 우선 티케팅, 추가 수하물 허용, 라운지 이용 등의 다양한 혜택을 누리며 나아가 카타르 항공과 호텔, 렌터카, 여행사 등의 파트너사에서 축적한 Qmile을 이용하여 혜택을 극대화 시킬 수 있다.

② 승무원 인재상

• 카타르 항공의 승무원은 중동 항공사 최고의 승무원으로 인정받고 있다.
• 2003년부터 5년 연속 '중동 최고의 승무원'으로 선정되었고, '세계 최고의 승무원' 부분에서 2위에 오르면서 세계적으로 인정받는 승무원의 위치를 갖게 되었다.
• 카타르 항공은 Warmth(따뜻함), Charisma(카리스마), Professionalism(프로정신)을 갖춘 80여 개국 출신의 인재를 전 세계에서 채용하고 있다.

③ 항공기 보유 상황

• 2019년 4월 현재(185대보유)
• B777-200LR 9대

- B777-300ER 48대
- B777F 15대
- B787-8 30대
- B787-9 30대 오더
- A319-100LR 2대
- A320-200 34대
- A321-200 6대
- A330-200 14대
- A330-300 13대
- A340 4대
- A350 38대

④ Codeshare Partners

- ANA(All Nippon Airways), Asiana Airlines, BMI(British Midland), Lufthansa, Malaysia Airlines, MEA, Philippine Airlines, Saudi Arabian Airlines, United

⑤ 수상 내역

- **February 2008** : 매해 개최되는 Airport Expansion Middle East award에서 도하 국제공항이 Best Airport Airline partnership award 수상

- **December 2007** : World Travel Awards 2007에서 기내식 World's Leading Business Class Airline(세계 최고의 비즈니스 클래스상), World's Best Inflight Meal Service(세계 최고의 기내식상), Leading Business Class Airline In The Middle East(중동 최고의 비즈니스 클래스상) 등의 3개 부문 수상

- **July 2007** : 영국 Skytrax가 선정한 Best First Class in the World(최고의 퍼스트 클래스상), Best Middle East airline for second year running(2년 연속 중동 최고의 항공사상), and Best Cabin Crew in the Middle East(5년 연속 중동 최고의 승무원상) 등 3개 부문 수상

자격조건	<ul><li>만 21세 이상</li><li>고등학교 졸업 이상자</li><li>영어 회화 및 작문 가능자</li><li>암리치 212cm 이상(여자:발꿈치 들고)</li><li>해외여행에 결격사유가 없는 자</li></ul>
채용절차 (2019년 4월 현재)	• 1차 : 그룹 면접 ➡ 2차 : 필기 시험 / 그룹 토의 ➡ 3차 : 최종 개별 인터뷰
베이스	• 도하

지상직 승무원

출처 : Qatar Airways 인스타그램

근무형태	• 정규직
자격조건	• 조인하는 시점 만 20세 이상 • 고졸 이상의 학력 • 영어 능통자
근무요건	• Customer Service Agent
지상직 직원의 업무	• Check-in Counter, Boarding assist, 출도착, Baggage Service, Lobby, Transfer Desk, Transit hotel accommodation desk, Coach releasing, MASS
근무시간	• Shift work - 4교대 • 5days work, 2days off • 매달 스케줄이 issue • 고정 shift가 아닌 계속 바뀌는 근무 시간
복리후생	• 주택보조, 차량 지원, 유니폼 및 세탁, 의료보험, 휴가 무료 티켓, 카타르 항공 본인 이용시 ID90 무제한, 결연항공사 할인 항공 티켓, 부모님, 형제 및 직계 가족 카타르 항공 ID90 10회 지원, 결연항공사 할인 항공 티켓 • ERP(Exchange Rate Protection) : 환율의 급변동이 있을 경우 보장 • 도하 공항 면세점 20% 할인 및 도하 주요 호텔에서 10~50% 할인 등
채용절차	• 서류전형 → 1차 면접 → 스크리닝, 필기시험 최종 면접(1차 면접자에 한해 스크리닝 면접과 필기시험, 그리고 최종 면접까지 모두 볼 수 있음)

3 네덜란드 항공 (KLM Royal Dutch Airlines)

KLM은 네덜란드에 베이스를 둔 세계적인 항공사 중 하나이다. KLM 항공은 2004년 에어프랑스와 함께 AIR FRANCE KLM를 출범시키며 세계 최고 규모의 항공사 파트너쉽을 통해 세계 최고 규모의 여객 운송, 세계 2위의 화물 운송을 자랑하고 있다.

제1차 세계대전 이후 1919년 설립된 항공사로 1920년 암스테르담~런던선의 운항을 시작으로 현재 AIR FRANCE KLM의 전략은 One Group, Two Airlines, Three Core Activities(하나의 그룹, 두 개의 항공사, 세 가지의 중요 활동영역)이다. 이를 바탕으로 두 항공사는 각자의 독립적 네트워크를 구축하고, 상호간의 공조와 협력관계 형성을 바탕으로 세계적 네트워크로 확장시켰다.

KLM 항공의 경우는 2011년 기준 136곳을 취하고 있다.(자회사 화물 포함)

나아가 KLM과 Air France는 SKYTEAM의 멤버로서 11개의 다른 항공사와의 공조로 고객에게 세계 최대의 편리한 네트워크를 제공하고 있다.

출처 : KLM 인스타그램

① 항공기 보유 현황

- 2016년 4월 기준(123대 보유, 17대 오더)
- A330-200 8대
- A330-300 5대
- A350-900(7대 오더)
- B737-700 17대
- B737-800 30대(1대 오더)
- B737-900 5대
- B747-400 3대
- B747-400M 8대
- B777-200ER 15대
- B777-300ER 14대
- B787-9 13대
- B787-10(8대 오더 후 기존 B787-9 주문 변경한 상태 2019년부터 2023년까지 순차적으로 도입 예정)
- B747-400ERF 3대

② SkyTeam alliance(스카이팀)

　세계 두 번째로 큰 규모의 항공사 동맹체인 스카이팀의 멤버인 KLM은 Aeroflot, Aeromexico, Air France, Alitalia, Continental Airlines, CSAE, Delta, Korean Air, Northweat Airline, CHina Southern 등의 11개의 항공사와 함께 전 세계적인 네트워크를 구축하고 있다.

③ 승무원 인재상

　회사로서의 KLM은 사원들로 하여금 최대한 오래 회사와 함께 하는 것이 가능하게 하는 것에 목표를 두고 있다. 이를 위해 KLM 항공은 사원들의 융통성, 유동성, 참여

도, 그리고 건강에 특별한 관심을 가지고 있다. KLM은 '기대 이상의 그 무엇(Something extra)'을 할 수 있는 인재를 찾고 있다.

이는 항공업계의 다이나믹함을 이해하고, 변화를 두려워하지 않으며 스스로 동기부여가 되어있는 승무원을 채용하고자 하는 이유이다.

자격조건	• 영어 능통자(상황에 관계없이 영어로 대화 가능자) • 성별 무관 • 만 21세 이상 • 한국 국적으로 한국 여권 소지자(외국국적 보유자 지원 불가) • 승무원직 수행에 적합한 신체조건(키 158cm 이상 190cm 이하 기준) • 교정시력 1.0 이상 • 학력 무관(기 졸업자 및 졸업 예정자) • 수영능력 보유자 • 해외여행 및 신체검사 기준에 결격사유 없는 자
채용절차	• 1차 : 서류 심사 ➡ 2차 : 한국어/영어 인터뷰 ➡ 3차 : 최종 면접
베이스	• 서울

4 루프트한자(Lufthansa)

독일항공사인 루프트한자는 스타 얼라이언스(타이 항공, 싱가포르 항공, 유나이티드 항공, ANA, 뉴질랜드 항공, SAS, 캐나다 항공, 오스트리아 항공, 루프트한자, 바리그 항공, 라우다 항공, 티롤리언 항공, US 에어웨이즈, 브리티시 미들랜드, 아시아나 항공으로 구성된 가장 큰 항공 동맹이며 1997년 5월14일에 시작되었다.) 창립멤버로써 세계 10대 항공사 중 하나로 2002년 국제선 여객부분 세계 3위를 차지하는 영향력 있는 항공사이다. 루프트한자는 1926년 창설한 후 1945년에 폐쇄하는 어려움을 겪기도 하였으나 1953년 재창설 하였고 "자신만의 장점을 통한 성장정책"을 내세우며 발전에 고속을 가하였다. 1991년에는 항공기편을 120편에서 270편으로 대폭 늘리며 1994년에 민영화 기업으로 새로 태어났다.루프트한자는 유럽 최대 규모의 항공사 이자 루프트한자 그룹 내 최대 항공사이며, 현재 4개 대륙에 걸쳐 73개국 165개 목적지에 취항하고 있다. 루프트한자는 쾰른에 본사를 두고 있고, 프랑크푸르트, 뮌헨 및 뒤셀도르프에 허브를 갖추고 있다.

루프트한자는 업계에서 가장 환경 친화적인 여객기로 손꼽히는 보잉 747-8과 Airbus A380을 장거리 항공편에 투입하고 있다. 루프트한자는 유럽 내에서 A380을 가장 많이 운항하고 있으며 신종 항공기인 보잉 747-8도 업계에서 처음으로 도입했다. 루프트한자는 총 424대의 항공기를 보유하고 있고, 2015부터 2025년 사이에 225대를 증편할 예정이다.

출처 : Lufthansa 인스타그램

항공 화물분야 1위, 연간매출 약 150억불, 여객기 평균기령 5.5년으로 세계 1위, 정시 운항율 세계 1위를 자랑하는 루프트한자는 현재 432대의 비행기를 가지고 있으며 78개국 192개 도시에 취항 중이다. 매주 14,000번의 비행이 이뤄지고 있으며 전 세계적으로 94,000명의 직원이 루프트한자를 위해 일하고 있다.

자격조건	• 4년제 대학교 졸업 및 예정자 • 만 18세 이상 • 키 160cm 이상 • 해외여행에 결격사유가 없는 자 • 최소 25m수영 가능자 • 영어(상), 독일어 능통자 우대
채용절차	• 1차 : 온라인 서류전형 및 영어테스트 ➡ 2차 : 그룹 면접(개별 질문 포함, 기내방송문 읽기) ➡ 3차(최종) : 한국어,영어인터뷰, 롤플레이 ➡ 4차 : 신체검사
베이스	프랑크푸르트

5 핀란드 항공(Finnair)

1923년 11월 1일에 설립되어진 세계에서 가장 오래된 핀란드 국영항공사이다.

Finnair는 현재 직항편이 없는 유럽 도시와 아시아 주요 허브를 잇는 가장 빠르고 가장 환경 친화적이며 가장 편안한 연결편을 제공하고 있다.

아시아의 취항지로는 인도의 델리, 뭄바이, 중국의 베이징, 상하이, 홍콩, 광저우, 일본의 도쿄, 오사카, 나고야, 방콕의 태국이 있다. 2008년 봄에는 서울에 비행을 취항함으로써 핀에어 아시아 취항 지역, 운항 빈도 및 유럽의 연결편 수는 앞으로 더욱 늘어날 예정이다.

핀에어의 유럽 노선은 매일 수차례 운항하며 스케쥴은 아시아로의 빠른 연결편을 제공하며 만들어졌다. 핀에어의 가장 최근 유럽 내 취항지는 류블랴냐, 부쿠레슈티, 단치히와 리스본이다. 국내선으로는 14도시로 취항하며 국내 노선들은 적은 인구에 비하면 세계에서 가장 조밀한 네트워크를 가지고 있다.

핀에어는 지금도 유럽에서 가장 젊고 친환경적인 비행기를 사용하고 있으며 비행기 평균수명은 4년이다.

다가올 10년 동안 핀에어는 정기 여객편에 3종류의 항공기, 광동체 에어버스, 단거리 노선의 A320, embraer170/190로 운항될 예정이다.

출처 : feelfinnair 인스타그램

자격조건	• 고졸 이상 • 만 22세 이상 • 160cm 이상 • 교정 시력 0.7 이상 • 청각 및 중추 신경계 이상 없는 자 • 색맹, 색약, 이비인후과 질환이 없는 자 • 수영능력 40m 이상 가능한 자 • 영어능력이 능통한 자 • 해외여행에 결격사유가 없는 자 • 경력자 우대
채용절차	• 서류심사 → 1차 : 통질문 → 2차 : 수영테스트 → 3차 : 기내방송문 낭독, 지원서 개별질문
베이스	한국

6 싱가포르 항공(Singapore Airlines)

1947년 5월 민간자본으로 설립한 Malayan Airways가 싱가포르와 쿠알라룸프르, 이포, 페낭 간 운항으로 출발한 싱가포르 항공은 1965년 말레이시아연방 성립과 함께 말레이시아 항공으로 개편하였다. 그 후 1965년 싱가포르 독립과 함께 1967년 말레이시아, 싱가포르 양국 정부가 공동 경영하는 말레이시아 싱가포르 항공(Malaysia-Singapore Airlines)으로 재출발하였고, 1972년 10월 Malayan Airlines system(현 Malaysia Airlines)과 Singapore Airlines으로 분리 독립되었다. 싱가포르 항공은 제2차 세계대전 종결과 함께 아시아 지역에서는 가장 먼저 항공업에 진출한 항공사였다.

차세대 기종으로 '하늘의 호텔'이라 불리우며 현재 많은 관심을 받고 있는 초대형 항공기 Airbus A380을 항공사 최초로 도입하여 항공업계를 나아가 세계인의 관심 속에서 성공적으로 시범 비행을 마치고 현재는 싱가포르-시드니 노선과 싱가포르-런던(히드로) 노선을 운항 중에 있다. 이처럼 싱가포르 항공은 특유의 혁신정신과 반세기 동안 꾸준히 축적된 노하우를 바탕으로 항공업계를 선도하고 있다.

또한 싱가포르 항공은 일명 "하늘을 나는 궁전"이란 애칭이 있을 만큼 최신형 대형 항공기와 이에 걸맞는 세계 최상급의 서비스로 알려져 있다.

출처 : singaporeair 인스타그램

이코노미석에도 기내서비스를 최초로 제공하기 시작한 항공사이기도 하며, 이에 그치지 않고 지금까지도 다양한 서비스를 소개하고 또 질이 좋은 서비스로 고객들의 사랑을 받고 있는 항공사이기도 하다.

① 승무원 인재상

싱가포르 항공의 최고 수준의 서비스 제공 항공사로서의 브랜드 가치는 바로 'Singapore Girl' 로 불리는 싱가포르 승무원들로 비롯되었다고 할 수 있다. 싱가포르 항공의 특성화된 고품격 서비스와 고객 관리의 상징인 승무원은 그 만큼의 완벽한 서비스의 자세로 그 기대치에 부응하고 있다. 이에 따뜻함과 친절함을 바탕으로 다가가는 고객 서비스를 제공할 수 있는 인재를 채용하고 있다.

② 싱가포르 항공의 마일리지 프로그램(Frequent Flyer Program)

(1) Kris Flyer(크리스 플라이어)

싱가포르 항공의 마일리지 프로그램인 크리스 플라이어를 통해서 승객들은 원하는 여행지로 가는 무료 항공권을 받고 좌석 승급 및 가족이나 친구를 위한 동반자 항공권을 받을 수 있는 마일리지를 적립할 수 있다.

(2) Star Alliance(스타얼라이언스)

싱가포르 항공이 소속된 스타얼라이언스는 세계 최초, 그리고 최대의 항공 동맹 체로서 Air Canada, Air New Zealand, ANA, Asisna Airline, Austrian, BMI, Lot Polish Airlines, Lufthansa, Scandinavian airline, Spanair, Swiss, Tap Portugal, Thai Airways, United Airlines, US Airways, Vario, Singapore Airlines, Air China, Shanghai Airlines, Turkish Airlines 등의 회원사 간의 네트워크 공유를 통하여 전 세계적으로 162개국 841 곳의 취항 노선을 운항하고 있다. 스타얼라이언스는 상호 공존 및 협약을 통해서 고객들에게 전 세계 620여 곳의 공항라운지 이용, 회원사

상호간의 마일리지 또는 포인트 적립 및 사용을 통하여 전 세계 어느 공항에서든지 특별 회원으로 인정받도록 다양한 서비스를 제공하고 있다. 또한 향후 회원 예정 항공사로는 에어 인디아·이집트 항공·콘티넨탈 항공 등이 있다.

자격조건	• 키 : 158cm 이상 • 나이 : 제한 없음 • 학력 : 4년제 이상 • 시력 : 교정시력 1.0 이상 • 해외여행 결격 사유가 없는 자 • 영어 : 능통자 • 서비스 분야 경험자 선호
채용절차	• 1차 :온라인 서류전형 ➡ 2차 : 비디오 인터뷰 ➡ 3차 : 그룹디스커션, 파트너 소개 ➡ 4차 : 최종면접 및 스카체크, 케바야 입어보기 신체검사
베이스	• 싱가폴

7 캐세이 퍼시픽 항공(Cathay Pacific Airlines)

홍콩의 민간 국제 항공회사 캐세이 퍼시픽은 CX라고도 불리며 한국에는 1961년부터 진출하였다. 1979년 중반에 보잉 747-200기를 처음으로 도입하였고, 곧 런던 취항을 시작하였다. 케세이 퍼시픽은 노스트 웨스트 항공에 이어 우리나라에 두 번째로 취항한 외국 항공사로써 아시아 경제 중심인 홍콩에 베이스를 취하면서 뛰어난 지리적 조건으로 세계적인 항공사로 발돋움할 수 있었다.

세계 37개국 113개 도시로 취항하는 캐세이 퍼시픽은 아시아 지역 내 30개 도시로 편리한 연결이 되어있으며 one world(American Airlines, British Airlines, Cathay Pacific Airline, Finnair, Iberia, Lan, Qantas, Air Lingus) 제휴사와 전 세계 150개국 700개 도시로 글로벌 네트워크를 형성하고 있다. A340-600, A330-300 포함하여 100여개에 가까운 비행기를 소유하고 있는 캐세이 퍼시픽 항공사는 'I can fly(난 날 수 있다.)' 라는 슬로건과 "현대적인 아시아의 항공사"로 우뚝 서자는 회사의 브랜드 전략, "마음에서 우러나오는 정성스런 서비스"를 내세우며 회사 경쟁력을 높였다.

출처 : Cathay Pacific Airways 페이스북

캐세이 퍼시픽 항공은 최신 항공기를 보유하기 위해 대대적인 항공기 교체 프로젝트를 실시하였고, 1990년 중반에는 세계에서 평균기령이 가장 낮은 항공기를 보유한 항공사 중 하나가 되기도 하였다. 캐세이 퍼시픽 한국 승무원들은 일반적으로 서울을 중심으로 탑승하는 타 항공사와 달리 세계 전체 취항노선을 운항한다.

자격조건	• 학력 : 대졸 이상 • 한국어, 영어 말하기 듣기 능통자 • 암리치 208cm 이상 • 나이 : 만 18세 이상 • 해외여행 및 신체검사 기준에 결격사유가 없는 자 • 서비스 경험자 선호 • 토익 LC, RC 각각 350점 이상
채용절차	• 온라인접수 ➡ 비디오 인터뷰 ➡ 최종면접 1:1 영어 인터뷰
베이스	홍콩

8 동방 항공(China Eastern Airlines)

중국 동방항공은 1987년 중국정부의 민항 상하이관리국에서 분리되어 설립되었다.

중국정부가 선정한 중국 50대 기업의 하나이며, 중국 항공사로서는 유일하게 뉴욕, 홍콩, 상하이의 3대 증권시장에 상장되어 있다. 항공운수업 외에 무역, 광고, 화물운송, 호텔, 기내 식품사업·여행·부동산업 등 20여 개의 단독 혹은 합자 형식의 투자기업을 소유하고 있으며, 보유기종은 A340-600, A340-300, A330-300, A330-200, A300-600R, A319, A320, A321, B737-300, B738, B747F 등 세계 선진의 항공기 수가 200여대에 이른다.

전 세계 주요 국가와 중국 국내 70여 개 도시에서 280여 개의 노선을 운항하고 있으며, 국내외 여러 곳에 지사를 설치·운영하고 있다. 한국에는 1992년 서울-상하이

출처 : Cathay Pacific Airways 페이스북

간 전세기 운항으로 처음 취항하였으며 한국의 지방공항 경유노선 특화라는 공격적 영업으로 고객수를 늘리고 있다. 2004년 4월 현재 양양-청주-상하이 노선, 상하이의 푸둥[浦東]-청주-양양 노선, 청주-제주 노선, 청주-선양[瀋陽] 노선 등 6개 노선에 취항하고 있고, 일주일에 여객기 32편, 화물기 2편을 운행하고 있다. 본사는 상하이 홍차오[虹橋] 국제공항에 있고, 한국지점은 서울특별시 강남구 신사동에 위치해 있다. 전 세계 100여개의 대형 항공운수기업 중 11위에 이르고 있으며, 현재 다각화 경영의 발전 전략과 강력한 경쟁력을 구비한 국제적 기업으로 발전하고 있다.

동방항공은 '안전운항', '편안한 기내 서비스'를 최우선으로 대고객 서비스를 제공하여 연속 3년 동안 민항 "운송서비스 품질 향상" 운동에서 1위를 차지하였으며, 중국품질관리협회에서 "전국소비자만족기업"으로 평가 받았다. 중국동방항공 로고 원 안의 파란색은 대해(大海) 또는 대지(大地)를 의미하고 빨간색은 창공 또는 태양을 의미한다.

그 중앙에 새의 형상은 제비로서 중국동방항공의 항공기를 상징한다. 전체적으로 중국동방항공의 미래 지향적이고 발전적인 기상을 상징하고 있다. IATA(International Air Transport Association : 국제항공운송협회) 코드는 MU, ICAO(International Civil Aviation Organization : 국제민간항공기구) 코드는 CES이다.

중국의 2008년에 WTO 가입과 베이징 올림픽 이후, 우리나라와 지리적 인접성, 문화적인 유사성과 중국의 경제성장에 힘입어 문화교류, 경제협력이나 무역시장이 활발히 확대되고 있어 향후 중국의 관광시장은 더욱 확대 성장할 것으로 기대되는바 현재 비행 중인 한국 승무원들의 좋은 이미지에 힘입어 더 많은 채용의 기회가 이루어질 수 있을 것으로 기대되는 항공사이다. 나아가 동방 항공은 비교적 저가의 항공운임으로 우리나라 항공운송 시장의 점유율을 높여가고 있으며, 국제선 노선도 꾸준히 확대시키고 있어 아시아 1위 항공사로 성장할 수 있는 잠재력이 있는 항공사이다.

① 동방항공의 마일리지 프로그램(Frequent Flyer Program)

현재 케세이 퍼시픽이 중심이 되어 JAL, 베트남 에어라인 등의 많은 회원사를 거느리고 있는 아시아 마일즈 회원사이므로 마일리지 적립이 상당히 용이하다. 나아가 한국지점에서는 'Business Card' 혜택을 제공하고 있다. 이는 중국동방항공을

이용하는 승객에게 마일리지 누적이 아닌 이용 횟수만으로 서비스를 제공하는 제도로 한국 지점에서 자체적으로 만든 카드로서 중국에서는 체크가 불가하다. 중국동방항공 각 노선의 편도(한국/중국)를 9회 이용하시는 승객에게 일반석 편도 1회 (18회 이용시 비즈니스석 왕복 1회) 무료항공권을 제공함으로 고객 서비스를 위해 노력하고 있다.

자격조건	• 만 28세까지 • 2년제(여), 4년제(남) 대학 졸업자 • 키 162cm ~ 174cm • 나안시력 0.2 이상, 교정시력 1.0 이상 • 영어/중국어 능력자 우대 • 해외여행에 결격사유가 없는 자
채용절차	서류심사 ➡ 1차 : 한국어 / 영어 인터뷰 ➡ 2차 : 개별면접 ➡ 신체검사
베이스	서울

9 하이난 항공(Hainan Airlines)

출처 : singaporeair 인스타그램

설립년도	• 1989년
허브공항	• 베이징 수도 국제공항 / 하이커우 메이란 국제공항 / 싼야 펑황 국제공항
설립년도	• 129
취항지수	• 90
자격요건	• 만28세까지 • 2년제(여), 4년제(남) 대학졸업자 • 키162cm ~ 174cm • 나안시력0.2 이상, 교정시력1.0 이상 • 영어/중국어능력자우대 • 해외여행에 결격 사유가 없는 자
채용절차	• 서류심사 ➡ 1차 : 한국어/ 영어인터뷰 ➡ 2차 : 개별면접 ➡ 신체검사
베이스	• 서울

2

나라별 국제 매너

Tip

외국항공사의 경우 면접관이 다양한 국가에서 오기 때문에 각 나라별 매너를 숙지하고 있으면 면접시 도움이 될것이다.

 한국

1. 사람을 만났을 때에는 약간 고개를 숙여 인사한다.

2. 아래 사람이 위 사람에게 먼저 인사하며, 한국 여성을 만날 때는 여성이 먼저 악수를 청해야 할 수 있다.

3. 만일 외국 여성이 한국에 오면 외국여성이 먼저 남녀 구별 없이 악수를 청할 수 있다.

4. 만일 상대방의 이름을 모를 때는 선생님이라고 불러서 예의를 갖추어야 한다.

5. 윗사람에게는 건강에 대한 찬사를 보내라.

6. 가족을 중요시하므로 가족에 대한 이야기로 해라.

7. 공중장소에서는 대항하지 말아라.

8. 크게 웃을 때 입을 가리고 웃어라.

9. 대중 앞에서 코를 풀지 말아라.

10. 나이가 많은 사람이 실내로 들어올 때는 아랫사람은 반드시 일어나야 한다.

11. 상사나 웃어른과 대화할 때는 시선을 아래로 떨어뜨려 겸손한 자세를 위해야 한다.

12. 자신보다 나이가 많은 사람과 대화할 때는 주로 건강에 대한 이야기를 많이 한다.

13. 미국에서는 가정생활 이야기는 사생활이라 하여 화제를 올리기 싫어하지만, 한국에서는 가족에 대한 이야기를 해도 무난하다.

14. 정치이야기는 되도록 피하는 것이 좋다.

15. 공공장소에서 어떤 사람이 말을 했을 때 그 자리에서 즉시 반박을 해서는 안 된다.

16. 약속시간을 지키는 것이 좋다.

17. 대중 앞에서 큰소리로 웃는 것은 바람직하지 못하며 웃을 때는 입을 가리고 웃는다.

18. 코를 푸는 것도 삼가야 한다. 보이지 않는 곳에서는 코를 풀어도 무방하다.

19. 한국에서는 껴안는 것이 흔한 풍습이 아니므로 조심해야 한다.

20. 손님접대는 주로 호텔이나 식당으로 초청하여 대접한다. 집으로 초대받았을 때는 꽃이나 선물을 가지고 간다. 선물을 받을 때는 두 손으로 공손히 받고 상대방이 선물을 풀어보라고 하기 전에는 절대로 풀어서는 안 된다.

21. 한식은 코스가 아니라, 한상차림이 원칙이므로 음식은 한꺼번에 식탁에 차려진다. 그러므로 원하는 것을 적당히 덜어먹는 것이 좋다.

22. 사람을 만나거나 방문할 때 옷을 잘 차려 입으면 상대방을 존중해 주는 것으로 생각한다.

미국

1. 먼저 주제, 목적을 말하고 부연 설명을 나중에 하는 것이 일반화되어 있다.

2. 인종과 민족이 모여 사는 나라이므로 인종문제에 관한 화제는 피하도록 한다.

3. 식사, 음주 매너 등을 잘 지키도록 한다.

4. 공중 화장실은 동전을 넣어야 문이 열려 사용할 수 있으며, 사용 시에는 우리 나라와는 달리 화장실 입구에 줄을 서서 칸이 빌 때마다 차례로 이용한다.

5. 서로 근접했을 때 상대방을 계속 쳐다보지 않도록 한다.

6. 팔짱을 끼고 다니면 동성연애자로 오해를 받으므로 유의하도록 한다.

7. 지역의 해안가나 공원에서는 절대 금주이다.

8. 인 신상에 관한 질문은 피한다. (서구인에게 공통되는 사항)

9. 함께 식사를 할 때 초청한 분이 식사를 더 권유하면 비록 배가 부르더라도 조금 더 먹는 것이 공손함의 표시지만 서양에서는 "No, thanks" 라고 사양하는 것이 매너이다. 한국의 공손은 상대방의 체면을 올려주는 언어적 행위로 겸양의 의미가 강한 반면, 서양식 매너는 때와 장소와 상황(T.P.O : Time, Place, Occasion)에 맞는 행동으로 적절성을 강조한다.

아랍(중동)

1. 서울 인사동을 함께 쇼핑하거나 한국 민화를 선물할 때, 개가 그려진 민화를 권하거나 선물해서는 안 된다.

2. 손을 잡는 것은 우정과 존경을 표현하는 것이다.

3. 무슬림은 이슬람교 율법에 따라 와인을 마시지 않는다. 1999년 10월 이란 대통령이 프랑스를 국빈 방문하려던 때의 일이다. 이란 대통령은 이슬람 율법에 따라서 와인을 마실 수 없을 뿐만 아니라 와인이 나오는 자리에 참석할 수도 없다고 주장했다. 프랑스측은 와인이 없는 만찬은 상상할 수 없다고 반박해 결국 만찬은 취소됐다.

4. 무슬림들은 오직 알라(Allah)의 이름으로 거룩하게 잡은 고기만 먹기도 한다.

5. 초청을 여러 차례 거절한다.

6. 돼지고기를 먹지 않는다.

7. 여자가 혼자 있는 집을 방문할 수 없다.

8. 여인들이 뒷방에 있는 것, 가족의 다른 남자들과 함께 앉지 않는 것, 손님을 안방으로 모시는 것에 대하여 이상하게 여겨서는 안 된다.

9. 여자를 빤히 쳐다 보아서는 안 된다.

10. 남자는 여자가 먼저 악수를 청해 손을 내밀기 전에는 여자와 악수해서는 안 된다.

11. 왼손은 부정한 손으로 무슬림은 왼손으로 선물 혹은 음식물을 주거나 받아서는 안 된다.

12. 다리를 꼬며 앉을 수 없다.

13. 앉을 때는 발바닥이 다른 사람을 향하지 않아야 한다.

14. 성경에 대해 항상 예를 표해야 하며 이것들을 바닥에 버려둔다든지, 다른 책의 밑에 두어서는 안 된다. 무슬림은 코란에 대하여 항상 경건한 마음을 갖고 대해야 하며, 옷감으로 감싸 보관해야 한다. 그리고 코란을 열기 전 반듯이 종교적인 예로 손을 씻어야 한다.

15. 사람의 집, 물건들에 대하여 감탄하지 말며, 그 자녀들에 대해서도 감탄해서는 안 된다. 어떤 문화 속에서는 이러한 것을 악한 영의 욕심과 동일시하고 있다.

16. 인사하는 방법은 양쪽 볼에 키스하고, "May God be with you" 라는 말을 많이 한다.

17. 정치 이야기는 금물이며 사우디 여성에 대한 화제 또한 금물이다.

18. 시간은 되도록 지켜야 한다.

19. 식사할 때나 악수, 기타의 행동을 할 때 왼손은 사용금지이며 오른손만 사용해야 한다.

20. 발바닥이 상대방에게 보이지 않도록 앉아야 한다.

21. 술은 권할 수 없지만, 음식은 권하면 거절하지 말아야 한다.

22. 상대방 부인의 선물은 준비하지 말아야 한다. 오해를 받을 수 있다.

영국

1. 새로운 사람과 만날 때는, 어느 정도의 거리를 유지해 주는 것이 상대방의 공간을 존중해 주는 태도이다.

2. 상대방에게 명예존칭이 있을 경우, 아무리 친한 사이라도 대화 중에는 꼭 그 명칭을 사용해 주어야 한다. 그 외 경우, 상대방의 배려를 받기 전에는 꼭 성을 불러야 한다.

3. 남자는 여자가 먼저 손을 들기 전에는 악수를 청하는 것이 아니며, 새로운 사람과의 인사말은 "만나서 반갑습니다" 가 "안녕하십니까" 보다 좋다.

4. 친숙하지 않은 사람과의 대화 도중, 직업에 대한 얘기는 되도록이면 하지도 묻지도 않는 것이 좋고, 정치나 종교의 대한 말도 되도록이면 피하는 것이 좋다.

5. 영국 사람들과 거래 시 시간은 꼭 지켜야 한다.

6. 손을 주머니 안에 넣고 있는 것은 예의에 어긋나는 것이며, 되도록이면 상대방에게 손을 보이게 하는 것이 좋다.

7. 영국 사람들과 거래 시, 줄무늬 모양의 넥타이는 피하는 것이 좋다. 본의 아니게, 한 고장의 깃발을 뜻하게 되는 수도 있다.

8. 손으로 빅토리 사인을 할 경우, 절대로 손바닥이 안쪽으로 와서는 안 된다. 영국 사람들 사이에서는 이것이 욕이다.

9. 초대를 받아 집을 방문할 때에는 간단한 선물을 준비하는 것이 좋다. 하지만 너무 비싼 것은 상대방에게 부담을 주므로 피해야 한다. 선물은 저렴하면서 성의가 보이고 실용적이며, 받는 사람으로 하여금 준 사람을 생각하게 해 주는 것이 가장 적합하다.

독일

1. 시간은 반드시 지켜야 하며, 상대와 인사를 나눌 때 명함은 각자 주는 것보다 되도록 홀더(Holder)에 넣어서 주며 또는 회의가 끝난 다음에 준다.

2. 독일 사람들과 악수할 때는 신중히 성의 있게 해야 한다.

3. 상대를 호칭할 때 주로 성을 부르고 직위도 함께 불러주며 여성들에게 Mrs 혹은 Miss를 붙여준다.

4. 길을 걸을 때 오른쪽에서 걷는 사람이 윗사람이라는 것을 알아두어야 한다.

5. 모임이 끝나고 나올 때 제일 중요한 사람에게 먼저 인사해야 하고 모임 중에 가장 부드럽게 말하는 사람이 그 자리에서 가장 직위가 높은 사람이라고 생각하면 된다.

6. 대화는 취미와 스포츠 또는 독일에서 가본 곳에 대해 이야기하지만 2차 대전이나 가족에 대한 질문은 삼가야 한다.

7. 주머니에 손을 넣고 다니는 것은 겸손하지 못하다고 생각하며, 껌을 씹으면서 말하면 상대를 무시하는 것으로 여긴다.

8. 좋다는 것을 미소로 표현하지 않으며, 사업상의 말을 할 때는 문을 닫고 한다.

9. 자리에 앉으라고 할 때 앉아야 하며, 사교상의 이야기는 마지막 코스에 한다.

10. 백합과 장미는 선물하지 않는데 그 이유는 그 꽃들이 주로 장례식에 사용되기 때문이며, 특히 13송이는 피한다.

인도네시아

1. 인도네시아 사람은 처음 만날 때는 악수를 하지만 그 다음에는 하지 않는다. 그러나 먼 여행을 떠날 때는 악수를 한다.

2. 심장에 손을 대면 존경한다는 뜻이며, 직위를 중요시 여기기 때문에 직함을 되도록 불러준다.

3. 명함을 두 손으로 받고, 받은 다음 신중히 읽어봐야 하며, 지갑이나 뒷 주머니에 명함을 넣으면 안 된다.

4. 대화는 가족, 음식, 날씨, 여행 경험담 등을 나누어야 하며 실내에서는 신발을 벗어야 한다.

5. 인사할 때 껴안거나 볼 키스를 해서는 안 된다.

6. 길을 물어 보았을 때 잘 몰라도 대충 알려주므로 한 사람에게만 물어보지 말고 되도록 여러 사람에게 물어봐야 한다.

7. 선물을 받고는 글이나 말로써 고맙다는 표현을 해야 한다.

8. 먹을 때는 되도록 말은 하지 말고 더 먹으라고 할 때 먹어야 한다. 음식은 조금 남기는 것이 예의다.

9. 음식은 반드시 오른손으로 먹을 것이며 여자는 다른 테이블에서 먹을 수도 있다.

일본

1. 일본사람과 인사할 때는 허리를 굽힌다.

2. 아래 사람이 위 사람보다 허리를 더 구부려 오래 인사한다.

3. 직위가 같을 때도 나이가 더 많은 사람에게 예의를 갖추어 허리를 한 번 더 구부린다.

4. 상대를 부를 때 이름보다 성을 주로 부른다.

5. 명함을 항상 가지고 다녀야 하며, 명함에 한 면은 영어, 다른 면은 일본어를 인쇄해 넣어야 한다.

6. 명함을 줄 때는 두 손으로 공손히 주어야 하며, 명함은 받아서 탁자 위에 놓고 잘 살펴 보면서 계속 대화해야 한다.

7. 받은 명함을 뒷 주머니나 지갑에 넣지 말아야 한다.

8. 음식, 스포츠, 여행에 대해서 대화를 나누되 2차 대전과 사생활, 직장에 대한 질문은 삼가야 한다.

9. 특별히 할 말이 없을 땐 침묵이 안전하며, 혹 기분이 나빠도 미소를 지어라.

10. 친숙의 표시로 상대방의 등은 절대 두드리지 말고 대중석상에서는 코를 풀지 말아야 한다.

11. 시간은 항상 지켜야 하며, 집으로 초대 받으면 영광으로 생각하라.

12. 선물은 먹는 것 보다 오래 가지고 있을 수 있는 펜 셋트 종류로 하는 것이 좋다.

13. 젓가락을 음식 그릇에 올려놓거나 밥에 올려놓지 말고 방향이 상대방 쪽으로 가지 않도록 한다.

14. 술은 자신이 따라 마시지 말아야 하며, 상대가 따라줄 때는 두 손으로 잔을 받아야 한다.

15. 손님 잔이 비어있지 않도록 해야 한다.

16. 미국에서 하는 OK라는 사인은 그들에게 돈이란 뜻이다.

17. 호수를 행운이라고 생각한다.

18. 일본인은 냉정성을 중시한다. 일본인이 존경하는 대표적인 인격은 '냉정성'을 갖춘 사람이다.

19. 대부분 소식을 한다.

20. 짝으로 된 것이 행운을 준다고 여기므로 선물은 짝으로 된 세트를 주는 것이 좋다.

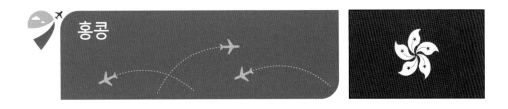

홍콩

1. 홍콩 사람을 만나면 허리를 굽혀 인사해야 하는데 높은 사람에게 제일 먼저 인사한다.

2. 두 손으로 명함을 주며 명함에 중국말로 써 넣어야 한다.

3. 대화 시 건강에 대한 질문과 사업이 어떠냐는 질문을 하지만 정치 이야기는 삼가 한다.

4. 대화 시 조금 멀리 떨어져야 하며, 사람을 만지는 것은 금물이다.

5. 상대를 껴안는다든가 등을 두드린다든가 해서는 안되며 남자는 다리를 꼬지 않는다.

6. 사업접대상 하는 식사모임에서는 8가지 내지 12가지 코스의 식사가 나온다.

7. 냅킨이 없고, 입을 닦아야 할 경우, 테이블 크로스를 사용한다.

8. 선물을 주는 것은 풍습이나 시계를 주면 죽음을 뜻한다.

9. 특히 똑딱똑딱하는 소리는 죽음을 재촉하는 소리라고 생각한다.

10. 선물은 준 사람이 열어 보라고 할 때 열어보는 것이 좋다.

사업상 오스트레일리아 사람들을 만날 때 꼭 알아두어야 할 사항들이 있다.

1. 오스트레일리아 사람들은 "Hello" 혹은 "Good day" 라는 말을 많이 쓴다.

2. 상대방의 명함은 잘 받으면서 자신의 명함은 상대방에게 주지 않는 편이다.

3. 옷은 점잖게 입으며, 상대의 직위를 별로 중요시 여기지 않는다.

4. 택시를 타면 주로 운전수 옆 좌석에 앉는다.

5. 그들은 사업상 사람을 만날 때 가벼운 이야기부터 시작한다.

6. 사업 이야기를 꺼내기 전에 간단한 주제(Small talk), 이를테면 스포츠나 여행에 관한 것들에 대해 편안하게 이야기한다.

7. 만일 만날 약속을 하고 시간을 어긴다면 개인뿐 아니라 회사에 까지 지장을 초래할 수 있다.

8. 오스트레일리아 사람들과 대화하면서 한국이나 미국에서처럼 엄지손가락을 펴서 상대방에게 최고라는 표시를 한다면 그것은 욕을 하는 것이나 다름없다.

9. Pub에 가서 "shouting for a round" 하면 자기가 다 계산한다는 뜻이다.

10. 저녁은 주로 6~8시 사이에 하고 몇 시간 지난 다음에 다시 서퍼(supper)라고 해서 또 먹는다.

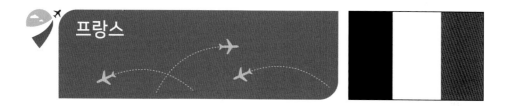

프랑스

1. 쉐프(Chef)가 한국에서는 주방장을 뜻하지만 블란서에서는 상관이라는 뜻이라는 점을 염두에 두어야 한다.

2. 프랑스인들은 타이틀을 중요시한다. 교수나 엔지니어에게 ○○○교수님이라든가 하는 타이틀을 붙여준다.

3. 친한 사이라도 격식을 따지며, 이름을 부를 때 성을 부른다. 앉아있을 때나 서 있을 때도 항상 손이 상대방에게 보여야 한다.

4. 대화는 음식, 문화, 다른 나라, 스포츠 등으로 시작해서 사업상 이야기는 식사가 끝난 다음에 한다.

5. 사업상 점심을 초대해도 무방하고 와인을 마셔도 괜찮다.

6. 집으로 초대받았을 때 꽃을 가져가도 좋으나 반드시 홀수로 사가야 하며 국화는 안 된다.

7. 물건의 가격, 원급 또는 가족에 대한 질문은 삼가해야 한다.

8. 식탁의 테이블 세팅에 빵 접시가 따로 없다.

9. 블란서 사람들은 먹기 위해 살고(live to eat), 미국사람들은 살기 위해 먹는다(eat to live)는 말이 나돌 정도로 식사를 중요시 한다.

베트남

1. 베트남 사람과 본인 사이에 침묵이 오랫동안 흐를 경우에 언짢게 생각할 필요는 없다. 왜냐하면 베트남 사람은 이러한 침묵을 일종의 상대방과 대화를 즐기고 있다는 것을 표현하는 한 방법으로 사용하기 때문이다.

2. 손가락을 튕겨 소리를 내는 행위 그리고 휘파람을 부는 행위를 베트남 사람들은 예의가 없는 행위라고 간주한다.

3. 애국심이 강한 편이라 자국에 대한 나쁜 이야기는 안 하는 편이 좋다.

4. 종교 이야기는 피하는 것이 좋다.

카자흐스탄

1. 문턱을 가운데 두고 악수하는 것은 피해야 한다.

2. 악수를 하며 인사하지 않는다.

3. 연장자를 부를 때는 이름과 오체스트바(이름 뒤에 붙이는 아버지 이름)를 같이 부르는 것이 예의이다.

중국

1. 대개 선물을 받기 전에 세 번 정도 거절하는 것이 예의이다.

2. 태평문(太平門), 자동차를 기차(汽車), 기차를 화차(火車)라고 하며 글자도 간자체를 많이 쓰인다.

3. 일본과는 달리 중국인들은 술자리에서 노래를 부르거나 술에 취해서 떠들지 않는다.

4. 자기가 사용하던 젓가락으로 음식을 집어 주는 습관이 있다.

5. 한자가 어렵다는 말보다는 의미가 있어서 흥미롭다는 말을 듣기 좋아한다.

6. 사람들은 붉은색을 선호한다.

캄보디아

1. 찍을 때 셋이 찍으면 가운데 사람이 일찍 죽는다고 생각한다. 그래서 셋이서 사진 찍는 것을 피하는 것을 보게 된다.

태국

1. 불교국으로 불상, 승려를 신성시하며, 왕가에 대한 존경심을 가지고 있다. 따라서 승려들의 몸이나 불상에 손을 대서는 안 되며, 이들을 욕되게 하는 언행은 용납되지 않는다.

2. 남의 머리를 만지지 않도록 한다. 어린이가 귀엽다고 머리를 쓰다듬어서는 안 된다.

3. 이름을 부르는 것이 정식이어서 이름 앞에 'Mr'나 'Miss'를 붙여 부른다.

4. 두 손을 턱 근처에서 배려하듯 모아서 하며 '와이(Wai)'라고 말한다.

5. 왕족에 대한 언급을 함부로 하지 말아야 한다. 왕 및 왕족의 사진을 한 손가락으로 가리키지 말아야 한다.

말레이시아

1. 이슬람교를 종교로 갖고 있는 사람들은 돼지고기를 먹지 않으며 개(犬)도 깨끗하지 못한 동물로 여겨 가까이 하지 않는다. 또한 왼손을 부정한 손으로 여기므로 식사를 하거나 악수를 하거나 물건을 건넬 때는 오른손을 사용한다.

2. 사람의 머리를 만져서는 안 된다.

3. 개는 부정함을 뜻하기 때문에 어린아이에게 주는 장난감 강아지나 개 그림이 들어간 선물 등은 모욕적인 행위로 받아들여진다.

3

Phonetic Alphabet

모든 항공기와 관제간 무선통신에 사용되는 음성 알파벳-항공 예약 시스템, 기내 등에서 사용된다. 항공용어에 기본이 되는 음성 알파벳을 알고 있으면 언젠가 외국 항공사 면접관에게 또는 교육을 받을 때 필요 시 스펠링을 불러줄 때에 활용할 수 있으므로 꼭 기억하도록 하자.

- Alpha
- Bravo
- Charlie

- Delta
- Echo
- Foxtrot(Father)

- Golf
- Hotel
- India

- Juliet
- Kilo
- Lima

- Mike
- November
- Oscar

- Papa
- Quebec
- Romeo

- Sierra(Smile)
- Tango
- Uniform

- Victor(Victory)
- Whiskey
- X-ray

- Yankee
- Zulu

Chapter 2

Key Points, Tips and Guidelines for Interview

Airline
English
Interview

영어 인터뷰의 포인트

① Smile

서비스의 기본인 스마일. 면접관이 나를 바라보지 않을 때나 당황스러운 질문을 하더라도 스마일을 유지하도록 노력한다.

② Eye-Contact

외국인 면접관이 있을 때에는 특별히 eye-contact에 신경 써야 한다. 눈을 계속 보고 있기 힘들 때는 수평적인 약간의 시선이동을 하고, 시선을 골고루 분산하도록 한다.

③ Communication Skill

최소한 외국인 승객과 의사소통을 할 정도의 영어 실력뿐 아니라 비언어적인 의사소통 능력, 그리고 Listening skill도 여기에 포함된다는 것을 잊지 말자.

④ Confidence

자신감 있는 목소리로 정확하고 밝게 힘 있게 말한다. 자신감이 있는 사람은 목소리가 활기차다. 목소리가 밝고 활기찬 사람은 여러 항목에서 좋은 평가를 받을 수 있다. 특히 외국항공사에서는 자신감이 아주 중요한 평가 항목 중 하나이다.

영어 인터뷰 시 유의사항

1. 면접관을 고객, 또는 함께 일할 동료로 생각하여 친절하게 긍정적으로 답변한다. 면접관은 고객의 입장에서 그리고 동료의 입장에서 지원자를 평가한다.

2. 목소리는 밝고 자신감 있는 태도로 답변한다.

3. 너무 과장된 손짓, 손을 만지작거리거나 머리를 만지는 등 불필요한 제스처는 금물이나 외국항공사의 경우 적절한 제스처를 사용함으로써 면접관을 이해시키는데 효과가 있을 수 있고 open-mind의 성격의 소유자로 보일 수 있다.

4. 이력서나 지원서에 작성한 내용과 반드시 일치하여 답변한다.

5. 질문에 대해 yes, no 등 one word로 대답하지 않고 because 등으로 연결하여 반드시 설명을 붙이도록 한다.

6. 면접관의 질문 요지를 잘 파악한다. 질문을 알아듣지 못했을 때는 질문의 요지를 다시 파악하여 엉뚱한 답변을 하지 않도록 한다. 영어로 인터뷰를 하다 보면 질문을 제대로 알아듣지 못해서 당황할 때가 있다. 이럴 경우 다시 한 번 말해 달라고 부탁을 하는 "Beg your pardon, sir(ma'am)?↗라고 하면 좋다. 인터뷰가 상당히 진전되어 있을 때에 한 두 마디의 말을 듣지 못했다면 "Pardon, sir(ma'am)?↗ 이라고만 해도 좋다. 물론 어느 경우에나 말끝을 올려야 한다. 또 잘못 들었으면 그 즉시 다시 물어야 한다. 동문서답은 인터뷰를 망치는 지름길이다. 또는 생각하는 척 하다가 "What?"이라든가 "What did you say?"라고 천연덕스럽게 묻는 것은 면접관에게 불쾌한 인상을 주게 된다. 단어나 발음

을 알아듣지 못했거나 문장이 어려워서 질문의 내용을 정확히 이해하지 못했을 때는 "I'm sorry I couldn't follow you. I'm afraid I didn't understand your question. Would you mind repeating it, sir(ma'am)?이라고 하면 되고, 또 다음과 같이 말해도 같은 뜻이 된다. "I didn't quite catch what you said. Would you please say that again, sir(ma'am)? 이러한 표현들은 발음 연습을 잘해 두었다가, 어떤 경우에라도 즉시 표현할 수 있도록 하는 것이 좋다.

7. 면접관이 말하는 도중에 말을 가로막지 않고 경청한다.

8. 면접관이 의도적으로 답변에 퉁명스럽게 대꾸 하거나 지원자의 답변 태도, 지망동기, 성실성에 대해 문제를 거론하기도 한다. 응시자의 대처능력을 알아보기 위한 것이니 면접 도중 실수를 하더라도 낙심하거나 당황하지 말고 끝까지 최선을 다한다.

9. 질문에 대해 거짓없이 일관성 있는 답변을 한다.

10. 어려운 단어보다 쉬운 단어를 이용하여 답변한다.

11. 면접을 마칠 때는 "It's been very nice to talk with you, sir."과 같은 인사로 마무리한다.

12. 외국항공사 면접에서 동양의 겸손의 미덕은 통하지 않는다. 지원자가 가지고 있는 장점을 최대한 자신감 있는 태도로 어필해야 할 것이다. 말을 하지 않아도 알 수 있을 것이라는 추측은 금물이다. 지원자가 말을 해야 면접관이 알 수 있다.

③ 외국항공사 인터뷰의 시작과 진행과정

① 1단계 - 인사교환

일단 인터뷰 상대를 만났을 때에는 그냥 "Good morning."이라고 하기보다는 미리 면접관의 이름을 알아두고 "Good morning, Ms. Smith."라고 하는 것이 훨씬 친근감 있게 들린다. 면접관의 이름을 몰랐을 땐 끝에 Sir 또는 ma'am을 붙이는 것을 잊지 말자. 모든 면접에서는 첫인상이 가장 중요하다. 면접관과 눈이 마주치고 10초 이내에 지원자가 먼저 인사를 건넨다면 훨씬 사교적인 성격으로 어필할 수 있어서 플러스 요인이 된다.

② 2단계 - 착석

면접관이 "Have a seat."이라고 말하기 전에는 앉지 않도록 한다. 앉으라는 권유를 받으면 "Thank you, sir(ma'am)"이라고 말하고 앉는다. 앉으면 허리를 등받이 깊숙이 밀착하

되, 기대지는 않도록 한다. 그리고 두 손은 무릎 위에 단정히 놓고 미소를 지으며 면접관의 눈이나 콧날을 응시한다.

③ 3단계 - 인터뷰의 시작

인터뷰에서 지나친 긴장은 가장 강한 적이다. 외국인 현지 면접관을 함께 일할 동료, 또는 나의 고객이라 생각하고 최대한 긴장을 풀고 친근하게 면접에 임하도록 한다. 영어 인터뷰에서 실패하는 원인으로는 지나친 긴장감, 침착성의 상실, 애매한 대답, 동문서답, 예의범절의 결여 등을 들 수 있다. 하지만 자신의 결점을 알고 이것을 어떻게 극복할 것인가를 미리 염두에 두고 있다면 영어 인터뷰를 원만하게 치를 수 있을 것이다.

④ 4단계 - 인터뷰의 종료

인터뷰가 끝나고 마지막 인사를 할 때에도 다시 한 번 입사의 의지를 표명한다. 그리고 "Thank you for your time." 또는 "I have enjoyed with you. Thank you."라는 인사의 말을 잊지 말아야 한다. 이때 인터뷰의 결과를 언제 알 수 있느냐는 식의 질문을 하면 오히려 어색한 느낌을 줄 수 있다.

외국항공사 승무원 영어 인터뷰 5가지 TIP

① 자기소개는 철저히 준비할 것

영어 인터뷰의 시작은 자기소개를 철저히 준비하는 데에 있다. 자기소개는 모든 영어 인터뷰의 기본으로 이에 대한 완벽한 준비는 면접에 들어가기 전 자신감을 상승시키는 효과도 있다. 자기소개와 주요 이력 정도는 수백 번의 연습을 거쳐 자연스럽게 말할 수 있을 정도의 자기 것으로 만들어 놓는다.

② 반응 보이기

인터뷰 내내 면접관이 단답형 질문만을 쏟아내지는 않는다. 면접관이 조금이라도 길게 이야기하게 되는 경우 집중을 하되 표정과 함께 간단한 끄덕임과 "Yes", "Yep"과 같은 추임새로 자신이 경청하고 있음을 면접관에게 알리도록 하자.

③ 말은 천천히 그리고 또박 또박

우리나라식의 얼버무리기는 영어 인터뷰 최대의 적이다. 준비 부족으로 인하여 자신감을 잃고 속삭이듯 나열하는 문장은 누구라도 이해하기 힘들다. 짧은 문장이라도 자신감 있게 천천히 그리고 또박또박 말하자. 영어 인터뷰란 영어 능력뿐만 아니라 노력하는 자세와 영어에 대한 자신감을 테스트하는 것이기도 하다.

④ Sorry? Pardon?의 습관화

영어 인터뷰 중 모든 지원자들의 가장 큰 걱정거리는 바로 듣기(Listening)이다. 자신이 준비해간 것들을 전달하는 과정에서 예상하지 못한 질문이나 빠르고 어려운 단어로 질문을 해온다면 당황할 수 있다. 이에 대한 가장 잘못된 대응은 지레짐작으로 면접관의 질문 내용을 넘겨짚고 관련성이 없는 대답을 장황하게 늘어놓는 것이다. "다시 한 번 말씀해주시겠어요?"의 영어 표현인 Sorry나 Pardon 또는 "잘 이해하지 못하겠습니다. "I don't understand"라는 표현으로 면접관의 질문 내용을 다시 한 번 확인하는 것을 부끄럽게 생각하지 말자.

⑤ 항상 면접관의 눈을 보고 말할 것

외국 항공사 면접의 대부분의 경우는 한국인이 아닌 외국인 면접관으로 구성되어 있다. 따라서 영어권 대화 문화 중 가장 중요한 부분을 머리에 새기고 들어가자. 그것은 바로 "눈을 보고 대화하는 습관"이다. 외국에 나가본 사람들이 가장 어색해하고 당황하게 되는 것으로 외국에선 대체로 시선을 자연스럽게 주변으로 옮기는 우리나라와 달리 말을 할 때는 항상 상대방의 눈을 똑바로 쳐다보며 대화하는 것이 예의이다. 말을 할 때와 들을 때 시종일관 눈을 맞추자.

5

외국 항공사의 꼬리질문 방식

- So what did you exactly say to her? / Then how did she respond?
- How did you feel after she said so?
- Why did you do that?
- What did you learn from that experience?

이렇듯 끊임없이 직접화법을 유도하여 그 경험을 통해 배울 수 있었던 점까지 묻고 끝내는 경우가 많다. 유창한 영어 실력도 중요하지만 결국 답변을 통해 드러나는 지원자의 성격을 파악하기 위함이다.

6

외국항공사 면접 복장 및 메이크업

여권사이즈 사진을 찍을 때에는 긴 머리일 경우 올림머리, 단발일 경우 자켓 깃에 닿으면 안되고 이마의 3분의 2가 보여야 하며 귀가 보여야 한다. 메이크업은 화사하게 하는 것이 좋고 앞니를 보이고 활짝웃고 찍도록 한다.

에미레이트 항공의 경우 두가지 사진을 준비하여야 한다. 정장 사진과 캐주얼 복장 사진 두 가지가 필요하다. 승무원 복장 사진은 긴팔 자켓 정장 무릎밑 길이 스커트,

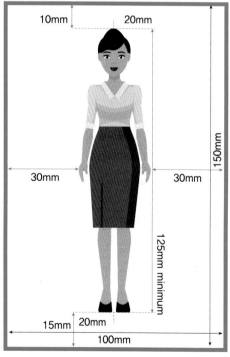
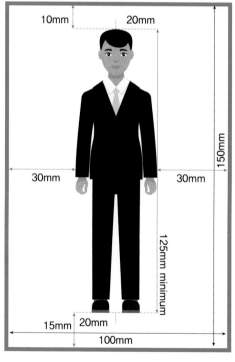

악세서리를 착용하고 찍으면 안된다. 사진 규정 사항을 꼼꼼히 확인 후 해당 항공사 사진 규정에 맞게 찍도록 한다.

카타르 항공의 경우 파란색 배경의 사진을 제출해야 하고 스커트는 무릎 밑으로 동방 항공의 경우 사진을 찍을 때에도 흰 블라우스 검정 스커트가 기본이며, 그 외 외국항공사 전신 사진은 정장 또는 화사한 색상의 반팔 블라우스와 스커트가 좋다. 면접용 구두는 기본 정장 구두를 신어야 하며 팔, 다리에 상처가 보이지 않아야 한다.

제출용 전신사진을 찍을 때에는 손은 주먹쥐지 말고 옆으로 가지런히 자연스럽게 펴야 한다. 발은 11자로 해야 한다. 다리를 교차하면 안되고 비스듬히 서도 안되니 주의한다. 앞니를 보이고 활짝 웃는 밝은 표정으로 찍어야 한다 면접 복

Formal photo
10cms × or 4" × 6"

Passport size photo

4.5cms × 3.5cms
or 1.78" × 1.38"

10cms × 15cms or 4" × 6"

10cms × 15cms
or 4" × 6"

장은 가장 기본이 스커트에 블라우스로 또는 치마 정장이며, 색깔, 무늬, 모양 및 머리모양에는 제한이 없고, 스타킹은 검은색은 피하고 커피 또는 살색을 착용해야 한다. 에미레이트 항공사 경우 화사한 색상, 오렌지, 핑크, 레드 계열등 본인을 살려 줄 수 있는 컬러의 자켓과 원피스 또는 탑과 스커트, 자켓을 입고 카타르 항공사는 반팔 복장으로 본인에게 잘 맞는 컬러 계열의 블라우스를 입으면 될 것이다. 스커트의 길이는 무릎을 덮는 기장이여야 한다. 소재는 상관 없으며 목을 가리는 스카프를 착용

해서는 안된다.

　메이크업은 카타르 항공의 경우 유니폼과 어울리는 진한 풀 메이크업을 선호하며 브라운, 버건디 계열의 아이쉐이도, 화사한 블러셔, 붉은 계열 립스틱, 마스카라 모두 꼼꼼히 메이크업 하는게 좋다. 카타르 승무원 메이크업 규정도 엄한 편이어서, 안되는 색조도 있다. 예를 들면 블루 계열 아이쉐이도나 누드 계열 립컬러등은 피해야 한다.지원자가 메이크업을 너무 연하게 해오면 면접관이 화장을 더해야 한다고 코멘트 줄 정도이다. 카타르 승무원 메이크업 규정을 보고 팁을 얻는 방법도 매우 좋으며, 본인의 강점을 살리고 약점을 보완해서 항공사가 추구하는 이미지를 만드는 메이크업으로 하도록 하자.

　에미레이트 항공의 경우 본인에게 잘 어울린다면 스모키 메이크업, 레드 계열 립스틱 등 색조를 진하게 해도 좋다. 주의할 점은 피부를 꼼꼼하게 보는 항공사이므로 피부톤을 화사하게 하되 목과 얼굴의 경계선이 없도록 하자. 메니큐어 색상은 레드계열이나 살색, 프렌치 네일을 선호한다. 카타르 면접에서 피부, 스카, 문신 체크 할 때 나중에 도하 올 경우 젤 네일을 하면 안된다고 코멘트 준다. 최근 특히 카타르 항공사에서는 피부 상태를 자세히 보며 최종 합격 후에도 노메이크업 사진을 요청 할 때도 있다. 면접시에도 그루밍에 신경을 많이 쓰고 가야 되며, 스스로가 관리 잘하고 그루밍에도 관심이 많은 지원자에게 더 호감을 갖게 될것이다.

양해를 구하고 위기를 넘기는 TIP

    면접을 하다보면 면접관의 말을 알아듣지 못하거나 혹은 이해하지 못하는 경우가 종종 생길 수 있다. 이럴 경우 당황하지 말고 질문의 내용을 다시 한 번 정확하게 되물어 파악하거나 생각할 시간을 달라고 하여 자신의 명확한 의견이나 답변을 제시하도록 한다.

① 생각할 시간이 좀 필요합니다만...

- Please let me have a time to think about it.
- I need some time to think about it.
- Could you give me some time to think about it?
- I need some time to about

② 이야기를 잘 알아듣지 못했을 때(되물을 때)

- Would you say that again, sir?
- I am sorry, I couldn't follow you.
- Sorry, I could not make that out.
- I am afraid I didn't understand what you are talking about.
- Would you mind saying it again, sir?

- Could you say that again?
- I beg your pardon, but would you repeat that again?
- I couldn't hear you. Could you speak more clearly?
- Would you speak a little louder?
- Could you spell it out for me?
- Could you say that in other words?

③ 대답은 정중하고 정확하게

- Yes, I do, sir(ma'am). / Yes, I have, sir(ma'am).
- I'm afraid, I don't (know), sir(ma'am). / I'm afraid not, sir(ma'am).

④ 본인의 실수에 대해

- Excuse me.
- I'm sorry.
- A thousand pardons for...

⑤ 상대방의 감사에 대한 응답

- You are (very / quite) welcome.
- My pleasure.
- Anytime.
- It's nothing at all.
- Don't mention it.
- Not at all.

Chapter 3

English Interview

Airline
English
Interview

Personal Data

Tip

주로 국내 항공사에서 물어볼 수 있는 간단한 신상에 대한 질문들이다. 간혹 외국 항공사 스크리닝 면접에서 물어보기도 한다. 간단한 질문이므로 단번에 잘 알아듣고 불필요하게 두 번 되묻지 않도록 유의한다.

1. When were you born? / Where were you born?

🎙 면접관의 발음을 주의 깊게 듣고 다른 답변을 하지 않도록 한다.

▶ I was born in 1996, Seoul. / I was born on the 10th of November, 1996.

2. Where are you from?

▶ I'm from Seoul. / I was born in Busan and raised in Seoul.

3. How many are there in your family?

▶ There are four members in my family, my parents, one elder sister and myself.

▶ There are five of us al together.

4. How long have you lived in Seoul?

🎙 이 질문은 외항사 면접 시 외국 또는 타지역에서 얼마나 살았는지로 물어볼 수 있다.

▶ I lived in Seoul since I was born. So, it has been more than 20 years. Currently, I live with my parents in Gangnam, which is located in southern part of Seoul.

5. Please introduce your family.

▶ My family consist of father, mother, older brother and me. My father is really attentive. He has ability in bowling and won a competition several times. My mother likes to read a book and listening to music. My brother is a high school student and he's good at math and science. We go to picnic every two times in a month. We are trying to spend time together at every night. That makes us feel closer and relax. I wish my family to be happy.

▶ There are _____ members in my family. (I am from small or big family.) Parents, one (two) older (younger) sister (brother) and myself. Father works for 직장명 혹은 회사 분야 company (is a 직업명 / runs his own business) and mother is a housewife. We have very close relationships together. Father is a _____. (직업, 아버지 이름은 생략할 것) He is a responsible / thoughtful / passionate / open minded person / a family man. Also, he is always busy but he tries to spend more time with family members.

6. Can you introduce your best friend?

🎙 친구 소개 = 자기 소개라고 생각하며 장점만 강조해야 한다.

▶ My best friend is _____. She is a _____. She is attractive / cute / good looking and sweet / friendly / considerate person. We've been best friends since _____ . We have many things in common.

▶ Her name is _____. She is same age as me and very pretty. She is positive, cheerful and very sweet. We have a lot in common. We meet at least twice a month and talk over coffee. We talk and share everything, and encourage each other. Everytime I meet her, I feel so happy.

7. Can you introduce your hometown?

🎤 서울을 제외하고 고향이 지방일 경우 물어볼 수 있다. 면접관이 외국인일 경우 음식, 쇼핑 등 여행객으로서 관심있는 부분을 함께 소개해 주면 좋다.

▶ My hometown is _____. It is located in _____, next to _____. It is famous for _____. It is the capital city of South Korea. It is the center of _____ and _____. (culture / economy / education / politics / business) Also, it has various sightseeing places, like _____ and _____.

8. Do you have any visible scar on your body?

🎤 이는 외국 항공사에서 스크리닝 면접 시 물어보는 질문이다. 눈에 보이는 상처는 반드시 없어야 하므로 답변은 한 가지임을 명심하자.

▶ No, I don't. Fortunately I haven't had any operation to leave visible scars on my body.

Small Talk

국내항공사의 경우 지시대로 열을 맞추어 들어가서 순서대로 인사를 한다. 외국항공사의 경우 외국인이 면접관이라면 눈이 마주치자마자 먼저 밝게 인사를 건네는 것이 좋다. "Good morning, sir, How are you today?"라고 먼저 인사를 하는 것이 훨씬 더 친절하게 보일 수 있다. 플러스 점수를 받고 시작하는 면접은 순조로울 수 밖에 없다. 하지만 면접관이 먼저 인사를 한 경우에는 "Thank you"와 함께 면접관에게도 인사를 건네보자. 간단하게 인사를 건네는 것만으로도 지원자의 태도나 사교적인 성격 등이 평가 될 수 있다. 또한 면접관이 "Please have a seat."이라고 할 때 자리에 착석한다. 인터뷰 질문이라기보다 질문자에게 친근감을 주는 대화법이 효과적이며 간단한 질문에 대한 순발력 및 위트 있는 답변, 그리고 면접관과의 공감대 형성이 면접자의 밝은 성격을 보여줄 수 있다.

1. How are you feeling? / How are you? / How are things?

면접실에 들어가자마자 지원자가 먼저 인사를 건네보자. 첫인상을 판단하는 것은 인사이다. 기본적으로 지원자의 성격이 친절하고 적극적으로 평가되므로 면접을 쉽고 원활하게 만드는 첫 단추이다.

▶ I'm fine, thank you. And you sir(ma'am)?

▶ It couldn't be better, sir. Thanks.

▶ I'm good but a little bit nervous.

▶ I'm very good, thank you, and how are you sir(ma'am)?

▶ I'm very well and excited to be here, thank you. How are you sir(ma'am)?

▶ I'm very happy to be here today. Thank you. It's great to meet you sir(ma'am)?

2. What is your full name / surname / first name / nick name?

🎙 주의해야 할 질문은 nickname에 관련된 것이다. 이는 보통 영어 이름을 묻는 질문이므로 불필요한 '별명'을 얘기하지 않도록 한다.

Surname / Family name / Last name / First name / given name / Nick name을 혼동하지 않도록 대답한다.

▶ My name is _____.

3. How do I call you? / How do I address you?

🎙 외국 항공사의 경우 물어볼 수 있다. 영어 이름이 있는 경우 영어 이름으로 얘기하는 것도 좋다.

▶ You can call me _____, sir.

4. Did you have a breakfast this morning? / What did you have?

🎙 간단한 질문이나 국내/외국 항공사에서 모두 물어볼 수 있다. 특히 외국 항공사의 경우 최종 면접에서 조차 간단한 질문으로 시작할 때 종종 사용된다. 아침 식사를 거르지 않음으로써 꾸준히 건강관리를 하고 있다는 인상을 주도록 하고 또한 한국음식인 경우 자연스럽게 음식에 대한 소개로 넘어가면서 면접관에게 소개할 수도 있으므로 음식뿐만 아니라 조리법, 재료, 식당 등에 관련된 정보도 함께 준비해 가는 것이 좋다. 쉽지만 연결고리를 어떻게 만드느냐에 따라 가점을 얻어낼 수 있는 중요한 질문이라고 할 수 있다.

▶ I had rice, Kimchi, and eggs which is Korean style meal. I always try not to skip breakfast for my health. Thanks for asking and How about you, sir/ma'am?

5. Did you come here alone?

🎙 부모님과 함께 왔더라도 그런 얘긴 자칫 독립심이 결여되어 보이니 굳이 꺼내지 않아야겠다. 다만 친구와 함께 지원해서 온거라면 얘길해도 좋다.

▶ Yes, I came here alone.

6. What time did you come?

🎙 이 또한 자신이 시간 약속을 잘 지키며 부지런한 사람이라는 인식을 상대방에게 전달해 줘야 한다. 조금 일찍 도착해서 다른 지원자들과 얘기도 하면서 긴장을 풀었다라는 답변도 좋겠다.

▶ I arrived here at 10 o'clock.

7. Are you nervous?

🎙 일반적으로 한쪽에만 치우치는 답변보다 조금 긴장되지만 괜찮다는 답변이 좋다.

▶ No, I feel more comfortable now after talking with some of the other candidates.

8. Are you comfortable with the uniform?

🎙 형식상 물어보는 질문이지만 당연히 그렇다라고 얘기해야 한다.

▶ Yes, I'm very comfortable and I think this uniform suits me.

9. What did you do before you came in?

🎙 간단한 질문이나 이를 통해 지원자의 성격을 알 수 있다. 다른 지원자와 이야기를 나누었다고 할 때에는 그 지원자의 긍정적인 면을 최대한 어필해준다. 면접관은 파트너 소개나 친구 소개 등을 통하여 지원자의 간접적인 '자기소개'를 듣고 있는 것이다.

▶ I had a small chat with another candidate. Her name is … She is attractive and such a lovely girl. We quickly became friends.

10. What time did you get up this morning?

🎙 지방에서 올라온 지원자의 경우 또는 먼 곳에 사는 경우 질문할 수 있다. 어떤 경우에도 피곤한 모습을 보여서는 안되며 자신이 부지런한 사람임을 간접적으로 어필해야 할 것이다.

▶ I got up around 7 o'clock this morning. I had to prepare myself for this interview and I didn't want be late, so I got up a bit early.

11. Where do you live?

🎙 위에 고향 소개에 관련된 질문의 답변처럼, 내가 사는 동네에 대해 간단한 자랑거리를 넣으면 좋다.

▶ I live in Hannam-dong, Seoul with my family. I have been living there since elementary school.

▶ I live in Jeonju. It is well-known for Bibimbap.

▶ I live in Busan. It is very far from Seoul. It takes about 5 hours to get there by car. Busan is located in the southern part of Korea, and it is the second-largest city in the country.

12. How long does it take to get here?

🎙 시간만 얘기하기보다 교통수단도 꼭 언급해야 한다.

▶ It takes about _____ minutes by bus / subway / train.

13. What time did you go to bed last night?

🎙 오늘 인터뷰가 걱정돼서 늦게 잤다는 답변보다 평상시 보다 일찍 잠자리에 들었다는게 스트레스 핸들링을 긍정적으로 하는 사람으로 보인다.

▶ I went to bed around _____ last night. It was a bit earlier than usual because I thought I needed a deep sleep for this interview.

14. What will you do after this interview?

🎙 많은 지원자들이 친구를 만나 오늘의 인터뷰에 대해 얘기할거라고 한다. 이는 자칫 면접관으로 하여금 오늘 면접에 대해 어떻게 생각하느냐, 평가를 해보라고 질문 받을 수 있으므로 주의하자.

▶ I will spend my day as usual. I'll have a lunch and go to an English institute. After that, I'll take a rest.

15. What will you do if you fail this interview?

🎙 당연한 이야기이겠지만 긍정적으로 생각하는 사람으로 비춰져야 할 것이다. 부족한 점을 보완하여 다시 이 항공사에 지원을 할 것이다라는 열정을 보여줘라.

▶ I think I would feel disappointed about the result. However, I'll try to find what I should develop and I'll try again next time.

16. What do you do on the weekend?

🎙 지원자의 평소 생활로 그 사람이 정적인 사람인지 활동적인 사람인지 알 수 있다. 면접관과 공통의 관심사를 언급한다면 면접이 즐겁고 유쾌해 질 것이다.

▶ I usually meet my friends. Whenever we meet we go shopping, somewhere like Dongdaemun. It's a very good place for shopping. Have you been there? (이 문장은 면접관이 외국인일 경우 사용해 보자. 지원자의 people skill이 보여질 수 있다.) It's famous for cheap and fashionable clothes. Usually I can bargain with people for cheaper prices on clothes. It's very interesting. Sometimes I go there just to look around. After that, we go to cafeteria and talk about everything. All of my friends are very sociable and humorous, so the time we spend together is really interesting. Sometimes, I invite some of my friends to my house and make some delicious food.

Personality

1. What is your personality? / What kind of person are you? / What kind of personality do you have? / How does the person closest to you describe you?

   ▶ I think I'm _____.

   ▶ My friends (professors, colleagues) tell me that I'm _____.

   ▶ My strong points are _____.

성격 표현 예시

- I believe I'm respectful, generous person and trying to establish meaningful relationship.

- My friends tell me that I'm friendly, considerable, outgoing and strong-willed person.

- I'm a hard worker, energetic, experienced, and patient. I have much strength so that I can perform excellent service at work.

- I'm an approachable person so I can easily make friends and make people feel comfortable with me. Also, I got a team spirit. So, I'm good at dealing with various passengers and making a good team work.

- I'm a good listener. People feel comfortable to talk to me. Also, many people told me that I'm very reliable person. I believe I can make my passengers feel comfortable with me.

- I believe that I'm honest and loyal in my relationship with others and that's my strong point. I also try to make time to get to know about my colleagues and support them if they need my help.

- I'm very active and cheerful. I usually don't have any trouble making new friends fast. And I've always been an optimistic person. It's really helped me in stressful situations and I usually resolve any difficulties quickly because I have optimistic and affirmative attitude. It's not always easy to keep such optimism, but I always try my best to do so.

- I always handle difficult thing with bright way, or look on the bright side rather than dark side. Last time I applied Korean Air and couldn't get a good result. But I found my weak point from that experience and studied harder than before to enhance my ability as a cabin crew. I think this attitude made me stronger.

- I can quickly accept different view from my own. From my experience, I've known well about how to understand others' character, thoughts and expression from what is different from mine.

- I like to be around people. I like making new friends. I'm a type of person who approaches first. I am good at concentrating and prefer to focus on one thing at a time. I'm not rigid. When I make decisions, I'm open to other possible options. That's why I'm said to be flexible. However, it doesn't mean that I'm indecisive. I always keep my options open. "Flexible, cooperative, and team player" are words that explain who I am.

- My friends often tell me that I'm a good listener. This listening skill will make a great contribution to your company because an ideal candidate for the position should always listen to what customers say and give the best possible service to them.

- My friends say that I am a self-started, highly motivated, and energetic person. I think I am outgoing and persuasive person and I can sacrifice my personal desire for teamwork. I'm willing to help other member. It's the first step for harmony with others. And I always try to understand others' feeling or condition.

- I tend to easily accept most of the things even if they are different from what I think they should be. That's why I can have a good relationship with anyone. I believe that this kind of communication skill will give me great advantage when it comes to building friendly relationship.

- My coworkers told me that I'm a good listener. They often came and asked me for some help. Whenever I hear about their problems, I always try to put myself in their shoes. My solution may not be the best but they trust me. And sometimes just telling me about the problems make them comfortable.

- I'm approachable person so I can easily make friends and make people feel comfortable with me. So, I am very good at team work. I believe this is one of the most important point to work as a cabin crew who should deal with various passengers and work as a team.

- I'm responsible person. I always try to fully in charge of my part and be reliable person to others. Whenever I have my duty or task, I do my best to complete it. So, I'm suitable person as a cabin crew who should always work as a team.

- I can quickly accept different view from my own. From my experience, I've known well about how to understand others' character, thoughts and expression from what is different from mine.

2. What's your weak point?

🎤 Lazy, careless, moody, hot-tempered와 같은 단어들은 삼가한다. 예를 들면 부탁을 잘 거절하지 못한다거나 완벽주의자 같은 단점은 서비스하는데 필요한 요소이기도 하므로 알려도 좋다. 양면성이 있는 단점이 좋으나 지원자가 직접 나의 단점이 장점이 될 수 있다는 설명은 삼가도록 한다. 단점을 알리되 그것을 극복하기 위해 어떤 노력을 하고 있는지 덧붙인다.

▶ I'm a typical workaholic. I don't mind working late at night. This character can be my weak point because I don't have enough time to exercise or relax. But I know good service also comes from good health and I'm trying to go to the gym for my health.

▶ I like to do things as perfectly as possible. I have a tendency to look at every detail and see if there's any way I can make it better. Some people have told me that this is unnecessary use of time, though they are impressed with the work I end up producing.

▶ I don't like to leave something half-done. I can't concentrate on something else until the first thing is finished. I never seem to be able to relax until I've finished.

▶ I can not leave things half done. Whenever I have any duty or task, I usually finish it very fast. So I've never heard I'm kind of lazy person. However, people told me I'm always too busy and in hurry. That's why I try to be more relaxed and detail-oriented person these days.

▶ I like to talk with people and get to know about them. So, I can easily make friends and have many people around me all the time. However. Sometimes I might seem that I'm more concentrate on talking with people than doing my work. So, when I work. I try not to speak too much and focus on my work.

3. What motto do you live by? / What is your philosophy in life? / What basic principle do you apply to your life?

🎙 좌우명, 생활철학이나 가훈에 대한 질문에는 Proverb(속담)이나 old-saying(격언)을 인용하는 것이 좋은 방법이다. 주로 국내 항공사에서만 나온다.

▶ I've been following one basic principle. The one thing that I always do is work hard, whatever I do. I always work hard with honest and generous mind. I also try to make time to help my colleagues and also to support them if they need my help with work.

▶ The one thing that I always do is work hard. No matter what I'm doing or where I'm at my personal life, I work hard to maintain a happy home as my job, I try to maintain strong relationship with colleagues and stay focused on the task at hand.

▶ The basic principles that I always try to follow are to be honest, generous and focused. Honesty is the best policy and you can't go wrong when you tell the truth or when you're honest with yourself about things. it's important to be generous with people in terms of your time and actions. In everything that I do, I try to be as focused as I can on the one task. Focused on something means you're putting in your best effort and working to complete the task efficiently and accurately.

▶ I never put off till tomorrow what I can do today. Putting things off just makes it worse later. So even if it seems hard to do at the beginning, I try to get it done and never let it goes.

Useful Proverbs

- Do to others as they would do to you.

  남에게 대접받고 싶은 만큼 대접하라.

- Honesty is the best policy.

  정직함이 최선의 방책이다.

- Do in Rome as the Romans do.

  로마에 가면 로마법을 따르라.

- Don't judge a man until you walked in his boots.

  그 사람의 입장이 되기 전에 함부로 판단하지 말라.

- Many hands make light work.

  백짓장도 맞들면 낫다.

- When one door shuts, another opens.

  하늘이 무너져도 솟아날 구멍이 있다.

- Better late than never.

  늦더라도 아무것도 하지 않는 것보다는 낫다.

- Well begun is half done.

  시작이 반이다.

- If at first you don't succeed, try again.

  첫 번째에 성공하지 못한다면 또 다시 시도하라.

- No sweat, no sweet. / No pains, no gains.

  노력 없이는 결실을 맺을 수 없다.

- Opportunity seldom knocks twice.

  기회는 왔을 때 잡아라.

- Nothing sought, nothing found.

  구하는 것이 없으면 찾는 것도 없다.

- A sound mind in a sound body.

  건강한 몸에 건강한 정신이 깃든다.

- Don't put off till tomorrow what you can do today.

  오늘 할 일을 내일로 미루지 말라.

- As ones sows, so shall he reap. / No root, no fruit.

  뿌린 만큼 거둔다.

- Where there is a will, there is a way.

  뜻이 있는 곳에 길이 있다.

- Life is a succession of lessons which must be lived to be understood.

  인생이란, 우리가 이 세상에 살면서 몸으로 배우지 않으면 안 되는 교훈의 연속이다.

- Early birds catch the worms.

  일찍 일어나는 새가 벌레를 잡는다.

- Everything comes to those who wait.

  기다리는 자에게 기회가 온다.

- In for a penny, in for a pound.

  한번 시작한 일은 끝장을 내라.

- Think of the end before you begin.

  시작하기 전에 끝을 생각하라.

- The awareness of our own strength makes us modest.

  자신의 능력을 인식하는 것이 곧 자신을 겸손하게 만드는 것이다.

- Never let your memories be greater than your dreams.

  과거에 만족하지 말고 꿈을 더 크게 가져라.

- The future depends on what we do in the present.

  미래는 현재 우리가 무엇을 하고 있는가에 달려있다.

- Diligence is the mother of good luck.

  근면은 행운의 어머니이다.

- One good turn deserves another.

  친절은 베풀면 돌아온다.

- Wisdom is more to be envied than riches.

  지혜는 재산보다 가치가 있다.

- Time and tide wait for no man.

  세월은 사람을 기다려주지 않는다.

- Behind the clouds is the sun still shining.

  구름 뒷편에도 태양은 빛나고 있다.

- Live to learn and learn to live.

  배우기 위해 살고, 살기 위해 배워라.

- If you laugh, blessings will come your way.

  웃으면 복이 온다.

- Do good and don't look back.

  선을 행하고 대가를 바라지 마라.

🎙 외국 항공사에서 특히 많이 물어보는 질문들이다. 이를 통해 지원자의 성격이나 인성, 가치관 까지 알 수 있기 때문에 최대한 긍정적이고 발전적이고 밝은 사람임을 어필해야 할 것이다.

1. What makes you upset/angry?

▶ I'm upset when I don't reach my plan to set up every day but, such a thing would pave the way that I can live harder for tomorrow.

▶ I'm upset to myself when I don't try hard enough in competitions.

▶ I actually get angry when I have to deal with rude or arrogant people. Especially in my team, I'm not very happy to work with my colleagues who are lazy and irresponsible. People who have irresponsibility in a team is hard to work with because this kind of behavior affects the whole team.

▶ Most of my friends say I'm a very easy-going person, so I'm not the person who gets angry easily. But sometimes feel uncomfortable when I can't keep a promise with myself. For example, I usually make a daily plan and try to complete the daily goal. But when I can't complete it, I feel uncomfortable and angry with myself. So I put on effort to make it even though a small goal.

2. What makes you happy?

▶ I feel happy when I choose desirable goals and make progress toward them.

▶ I always carry my family photo in my purse because it brings happiness and refreshing energy to me. So whenever I have a spare time, I frequently look at family photo, then I feel very happy.

3. What makes you sad?

▶ If I've let someone down or been careless with their feelings, I feel like I've failed. And that makes me sad.

Health Care / Stress / Sports

1. What do you do for your health? / What are you doing to keep your physical strength?

🎙 어떻게 건강관리를 하고 있는지, 그리고 승무원이 된다면 어떻게 체력을 유지할 것인지를 실내운동(indoor sports)과 야외 스포츠(outdoor sports) 각각 한가지씩 포함하여 답변한다.

건강관리에 관한 질문이라면 식습관이나 생활습관을 결부시킨다.

▶ I enjoy _____ (swimming, yoga, jazz dancing, jogging) twice (three times) a week. (I take a walk around the park / go hiking to the mountain near my house.)Also, I have a balanced diet. (have a regular lifestyle / have a fresh fruits and vegetables every day / try not to have fast foods.)

▶ To improve my physical strength, I try to go to the gym everyday even for 10 minutes. Thanks to my daily exercise routine, I have become physically and mentally fit.

▶ I drink about 7 cups of mineral water a day and try to have a balanced diet. And I go hiking and swim in the pool.

▶ I try not to eat too much. And I do simple aerobic at home and play badminton with my mom or friends.

2. How do you get rid of your stress?

🎙 스트레스는 누구나 받을 수 있다. 하지만 자신만의 푸는 방법이 있다면 이 또한 발전적이 될 수 있는 것이다. 그러므로 적극적으로 나만의 방법을 얘기하도록 한다.

▶ I let out my stress through scribbling. I write my thoughts and feelings on the paper. And sometimes I like to listen to music such as classic, jazz and new age. Sports like badminton, hiking also can be a good way to get rid of stress and it's really helpful.

▶ I usually meet my friends. We go to cafe to talk about everything. All of my friends are very nice, sociable and humorous so that the time we spend together is very interesting and relaxing.

▶ I personally think a certain degree of stress makes me alert. I also do yoga every other day and meditate for 5 minutes during the day. On weekends I meet friends and enjoy good food with them. This is how I stay level-headed and focoused.

3. Do you like playing sports?

🎙 스포츠에 관한 질문이라면 스포츠에 관심이 있다고 하고, 본인이 말한 스포츠의 유명한 선수나 경기방식에 대해 잘 알고 있어야 한다.

▶ Yes, I especially like baseball. / Yes, I like team sports such as volleyball.

▶ No, but I enjoy watching sports.

▶ No, I'm not much of an athlete, but I do like taking a walk.

4. What's your favorite sport?

▶ My favorite sport is _____. Actually, I don't know how to play it but I really enjoy watching it. If I have a chance, I want to learn how to play it. Also, my favorite _____ player is _____.

▶ I like tennis. I've enjoyed playing tennis since I was a little kid.

▶ My favorite sport is soccer. I did enjoy 2002 World-Cup in Korea and Japan. I prefer to watch together with my family and friends, shouting and jumping. Soccer can harmonize us.

▶ I like playing badminton and sometimes watching soccer games on TV. My favorite player is _____.

▶ I like swimming in summer and go skiing in winter. I'm good at skiing so I can teach how to ski.

5. Why do you like that sport?

▶ My favorite sport is Badminton, because it is easy to learn and convenient to play. I can play it anywhere if it's not windy. I play badminton with my parents after dinner because it's good for digestion and family unity.

6. Which do you prefer watching sports or playing sports?

▶ I like both.

▶ I enjoy playing sports more than watching them.

7. How often do you go bowling / swimming / fishing?

🎤 이 질문들은 보통 취미를 얘기하고 난 후 국내 항공사에서 추가로 물어볼 수 있는 질문들이다.

▶ I play about once a week. / 3 times a week / once a month.

▶ I go swimming almost every day.

8. Who is your favorite sport player?

🎤 스포츠를 좋아한다고 했을때 좋아하는 스포츠 스타가 됬다면 면접관과 공감 형성에 아주 좋을 것이다. 실례로 외국 항공사 면접에서 좋아하는 스포츠 스타가 면접관과 같아서 면접이 즐거웠으며 결과는 합격으로 이어진 경우가 있었다. 이처럼 취미 관련 부분에서 공통의 관심사가 생길 수도 있으므로 아주 중요한 부분이라 할 수 있겠다.

▶ My favorite sport player is _____. He (she) is one of the famous _____. player in Korea. (in the world) I like him (her) because he (she) is in good shape and one of the most professional player in his (her) field.

▶ I like Park, Ji-Sung the most. Since childhood, he has spent all his free time developing his skills in order to compensate for his lack of physical status. He is best known for his incredible durability in the game. He has been renowned for his good attitude and strong work ethic. He is an outstanding soccer player who has good sportsmanship and confidence in his games.

9. Do you work out?

🎤 이 질문은 운동을 하는가라는 질문이다. 혹 질문을 못알아 듣는 일이 없도록 주의하자.

▶ Yes, I go to the fitness center 3 days a week and do weight training.

10. Why do you play badminton?

🎤 이 질문은 배드민턴을 좋아한다고 했을 경우에 나오는 꼬리 질문이다.

▶ I play with mom or friends and that makes me energetic and happier.

11. Why do you like swimming?

🎤 수영을 좋아한다고 하면 이러한 꼬리 질문도 나올 수 있다.

▶ Swimming is less stressful on joints and bones than other sports.

운동과 관련된 문법 Tip 예시

- **Do 동사 + individual types**
  예 do yoga, do stretching

- **Play 동사 + 공을 가지고 팀으로 하는 경우**
  예 play baseball, play tennis, play badminton
  예외 do bowling

- **Go 동사 + ~ing로 끝나는 경우**
  예 go jogging, go swimming, go inline skating

- **It makes me + 형용사 구문**
  예 It makes me feel fresh when I do ~
  해당 구문으로 본인이 좋아하는 운동을 하고 난 후의 기분을 표현할 수 있다.

12. How long have you liked climbing?

🎤 등산을 좋아한다면 나올수 있는 꼬리 질문이다.

▶ I climbed Mt. Jiri with my friends when I was in the first grade of high school. It was hard to reach the top but the view from the mountain top was very beautiful and I could feel a sense of accomplishment. Since then I often go climbing mountains.

SPORTS		
• 조깅(jogging)	• 걷기(walking)	• 핸드볼(handball)
• 뛰기(running)	• 롤러스케이트(roller skating)	• 탁구(ping pong)
• 자전거(cycling)	• 스케이트보드(skateboarding)	• 스쿠버다이빙(scuba diving)
• 볼링(bowling)	• 승마(horseback riding)	• 골프(golf)
• 스쿼시(squash)	• 라켓볼(racquetball)	• 아이스하키(ice hockey)
• 농구(basketball)	• 수영(swimming)	• 권투(boxing)
• 미식축구(football)	• 축구(soccer)	• 배구(volleyball)

외국 항공사 추가질문 – Emotion-Related Questions

1. What makes you feel stressful?

🎤 외항사에서 스트레스에 관련된 질문은 답변에 유의해야 한다. 스트레스를 사람에게 받는다고 해선 안 된다. 답변을 잘 하는 사람들은 나 자신과 연결시킨 답변을 한다.

▶ I normally make the daily plans and try to keep those plans. But, sometimes, when I don't accomplish the daily plans, I get stressed out.

▶ Mostly I feel happy with everything in my life but I get stressed out when I have to start with something or when I have to deal with something that I'm not familiar with. For example, when I started to study English for the first time in my life, I was overwhelmed because I couldn't understand and speak, which frustrated me. As time passed by, however, I became used to it and got better. A and later I began to enjoy studying English doing my best to learn it.

2. How did you cope with work stress?

🎤 일하면서 받는 스트레스는 즉각적으로 풀 수 있는 것들(취미 활동…)이 없다. 하지만 외항사에서는 이러한 질문이 자주 나오므로 일하는 중에 스트레스를 받는다면 풀 수 있는 나만의 방법이 있어야 하겠다.

▶ I try to think myself that everything will be OK as time goes by and I will be able to work it out. All I need to do is just to focus on my job more. And I usually take a bath and have lemonade to get relaxed, reminding myself of happy memories. By doing that, I feel much better and fill myself of new energy to work tomorrow.

3. How did you manage stress in your work?

▶ Unless I have a lot of work to do that I just can't get away from, I make sure that I take my break time even for a few minutes. It is enough to keep me energized for the rest of my day.

4. Have you worked under stress to meet deadline? / How did you control your stress at that time?

🎙 이 질문은 Have you worked under pressure?로도 물어볼 수 있다. 마감 시간이 임박해 왔을때는 누구나 스트레스를 받는다. 어떻게 현명하게 극복하는지 예를 들어 경험담을 얘기해주면 쉽게 풀어 나갈 수 있다.

▶ When I worked at a restaurant, we got a reservation for a large group but we did not have enough time to get ready. Because my boss forgot to tell us about the reservation and when we were informed there were just 3hours left while we had to set 30 tables. So we were divided into two teams. One team for table setting, and the other for decoration. Things did not go as well as we had expected. But each group member worked hard. Thanks to our excellent teamwork and good communication, however, we made it on time.

5. If your colleague is in a stressful situation how could you help her to handle it?

🎙 동료를 도와준 예는 외항사 면접 시 항상 나오는 질문이다. 이 질문 또한 동료를 도와준 예로 활용할 수 있을 것이다. 이를 통해 본인의 경험담을 이야기해보라고 할 수도 있다.

▶ First of all, I'll listen carefully about her problem and help her to find out a better solution. I'll put my full empathy and think in her position. Then we'll eat some delicious food together and go to a singing room to sing and dance. Then she could be able to forget about the day.

Hobbies and interests

Tip

취미는 종종 그 사람의 성격이나 생활방식을 나타내주기도 한다. 그렇기에 단순히 취미만을 이야기할 것이 아니라 취미생활을 함으로써 얻는 것과 그것을 통하여 기쁨을 느끼고 만족해 한다는 인상을 주면 긍정적인 사람으로 평가될 수 있다. 예를 들어 배드민턴이 취미일 경우 날씨가 좋은 요즘 밖에서 누군가와 배드민턴을 치는 것은 큰 기쁨이라고 부연 설명을 해준다면 좋다. 항공사의 특성상 여성스러운 취미와 활동적인 취미를 하나씩 답하는 것이 좋다. 국내 항공사의 경우 노래 부르기나 춤추기 등은 그 자리에서 시킬 수도 있으니 자신 있는 것으로 준비한다.

1. **What do you do in your free time? / How do you spend your leisure time? / What do you do whenever you have spare time? / What is your hobby?**

   ▶ My hobby is swimming / doing yoga / taking photos / jogging / jumping rope. I've been enjoying it since _____ years back. (I was ___ years old / I was in 학교) It is really interesting and helps me to keep myself healthy. (helps me to release my stress.)

   ▶ On weekends, I usually spend time with my family, going to movies or going out to have delicious food. I also do a week's worth of washing, cleaning, and shopping. I love to cook and invite friends to dinner. It relieves the stress of work.

▶ I love to do many things for fun. My hobbies are reading books, watching movies, working out and many more. All of these really provide me with a great deal of entertainment and rejuvenation.

▶ My favorite hobby is listening to music and going to concerts. I especially like dance music. Last month, I went to _____'s concert and it was so much fun.

▶ I really enjoy watching movies. I love to watch all kinds of movies. Whenever a good movie is released, I go to a theatre and watch it as soon as possible. This is something that I enjoy very much during weekends. I think watching many different movies provides me a chance to think differently and widen my viewpoint toward our life.

▶ Walking along the river near my house. I try to walk at least 3km a day. Currently, I've decided to walk to my work place now that the weather is nice. The weather is beautiful and perfect for a walk.

▶ I love to go swimming whenever I have spare time because I think for me swimming is the best exercise because it helps me to stay fit and be healthy. I think I'm a good swimmer. I can swim about 100m free style without a break.

2. What's your favorite book?

🎙 음악, 영화, 책과 같은 관심사는 좋아하는 종류, 감명 깊었던 작품, 그리고 가장 좋아하는 배우, 작가, 음악가 등과 같은 질문이 나올 수 있다.

▶ My favorite book is _____, written by _____ from _____. This book is about the true love / power of positiveness / love between family members / true meaning of leadership / power of sharing mind / good way of communication. So, I could learn the importance of love / positive mind / leadership / sharing mind / communication in my life.

3. Could you tell me about that story? Why do you like it?

🎙 국내 항공사에서 나오는 2번 질문에 대한 꼬리 질문이다. 간단 명료하게 답변하되 배운 점도 가미해 준다면 좋을 것이다.

▶ The writer Joel Osteen offers unique insights and encouragement that can help me overcome every obstacle. He gives me a way to improve and helps me to experience victory, joy, and satisfaction in my life.

4. Who's your favorite author?

🎤 이 질문을 먼저한 후 좋아하는 책을 물어볼 수 있고 3번으로 꼬리 질문을 할 수 있다.

▶ My favorite author is Mark Twain.

5. What kind of books do you like?

▶ I like novel / fantasy / history.

▶ Autobiographies and biographies are so fascinating to me. I've read quite a few over the years. I love to read about the how people in these books fight to overcome their struggles in life. It helps me to keep fighting for what I believe in and to always stay strong.

6. What kind of music do you like?

🎤 음악을 좋아한다고 했을 경우 이 질문을 꼬리 질문으로 받는다. 외국 항공사의 경우 면접관이 먼저 음악을 따로 묻지는 않는다. 다만 지원자의 취미 활동 등으로 연결된 경우 구체적으로 물어볼 수 있다.

▶ I especially like (Christian/ classical / dance) music.

▶ I love world music. I have different CDs from India, France, China, Japan, etc. Although I don't understand them, I can feel their emotion. I think emotional touch is stronger than language. Among them, my favorite singer is OOO, the world's popular music band.

7. Who is your favorite singer and what's your favorite song?

🎤 이 또한 6번에서 언급한 것처럼 연결고리가 있는 질문이다. 국내 항공사의 경우 드물게는 시킬 수도 있으니 연습을 미리 하는 것이 좋다. 외국 항공사의 경우 면접관과 공통의 관심사로 흥미로운 면접이 될 수도 있다.

▶ My favorite song is "Hotel California" of Eagles. I like that comfortable melody and I can feel like traveling somewhere.

8. What kind of movie do you like?

🎙 의외로 영화에 관련된 질문은 외항사에서 많이 나온다. 가령 지원자가 취미로 영화 보기 또는 주말 계획으로 영화 보기 등 다양한 질문에서 답변이 나올 수 있다.

▶ I enjoy watching mysterious movie. Because it helps me to come up with creative ideas.

▶ I like romantic comedy (action / drama / fantasy / thriller) movies. Because, whenever I see those movies, I find them very interesting and I can get rid of all my stress.

9. What is your favorite movie?

🎙 8번과 마찬가지로 면접관과 좋아하는 영화가 같다던지, 아니면 면접관이 그 영화에 관심을 보이며 스토리를 물어보기도 하므로 공통의 관심사 형성에 좋은 주제이다. 다만 외국인이 면접관일 경우 그들도 이해할 수 있는 외화를 예로 들어야 할 것이다.

▶ My favorite movie is _____. Because, I like the story (I like the sound music / The story was really touching) and main actor / actress 000 is one of my favorite movie star.

10. Who is your favorite actor?

🎙 이는 외국 항공사에선 잘 물어보지 않는다. 다만 영화에 관련된 꼬리 질문으로 국내 항공사에서 물어볼 수 있다.

▶ I like _____. I think he understand and express his character perfectly.

▶ My favorite actor / actress is _____. She (He) is one of the most famous movie star in Korea. (throughout the world) I like her (him) because she is attractive (has a beautiful smile / is in good shape) Also, I like her (his) acting style.

11. What are your special skills? / What is your talent/ specialty? / What are you good at?

🎙 Special skill은 남들보다 잘 다룰 수 있는 악기나, 전공 이외의 구사 가능한 언어 등이 될 수 있다.

▶ I have a nursing experience and can take care of babies well. If I can be a cabin crew, I'll think babies are also my passengers and always try to take care of babies for their comfort.

▶ I can speak Spanish. When I was young, my family went to Spain and stayed for 1 year. I started to study Spanish and tried to spend time with Spanish friends. That made me to enhance Spanish skill.

▶ My specialty is _____ . I learned how to do (play, make) it when I was ___ years old. I think it's really interesting so I still enjoy it from time to time.

▶ Well, I wonder if this can be a specialty. but I can cook very well. I learn that from my mother. I like to help my mother with her housework. Especially at meal time, I always help her. I cooked Kimchi soup very well. It's a traditional Korean food that is but similar to stew. It tastes spicy and hot. When people compliment me on what I've cooked, I feel happy. I like being with people and cooking. So If you hire me, I can show you. I'd like to invite you to my house and prepare a lot of delicious Korean food, like Kimchi and Bulgogi. I would like to prepare a meal for you.

12. What food can you make?

🎤 취미가 요리라면, 좋아하거나 잘하는 요리의 만드는 방법을 간단하게 설명할 수 있어야 한다. 그 외에도 김치나 찌개와 같은 한국적인 요리의 조리법을 물어볼 수 있다.

▶ I'm a good cook. I can make a lot of different things like sweet and sour pork, Kimchi stew, and pasta.

13. Are you interested in cooking?

🎤 외항사의 경우 사람을 초대해서 음식을 만들었다라고 답변을 할 경우, 요리하는거 좋아하는지 이처럼 꼬리 질문을 받을 수 있다.

▶ Yes, I am. I enjoy cooking and I think I am a good cook. I often cook for my family.

▶ Yes, sir. I'm a pretty good cook. My mother taught me how to cook when I was growing up.

14. What's your favorite Korean food? What can you make?

🎙 이 질문은 외항사에서 한국 음식에 대한 꼬리 질문으로 나올 수 있다. 잘 준비한다면 면접관에게도 소개할 수 있으므로 친밀감 형성에 효과적인 질문이 되겠다. 그러므로 요리를 못하더라도 자신 있는 음식 한 개 정도는 소개할 수 있을 정도로 준비하도록 하자.

▶ My favorite is Kimchi Chigae. First, cut cabbage Kimchi into 3~4cm pieces. Second, cut all the pork into thin, suitable sized loaf. Third, add chopped garlic, salt, and sesame oil to loaf of pork. Finally, fry flavored pork on a cooker slightly and then fry with all the prepared Kimchi.

▶ Kimchi flat cake is my favorite. Cut stem part of Kimchi to 5~6 cm long and remove the moisture. Wash oyster and shrimp by shaking in salted water, and remove water. Chop small green onion to the same length of Kimchi. Mix Kimchi and small green spring onion with a big spoonful of sesame oil each. Put flour, sweet rice powder, egg, water and salt into a bowl, and stir it with bubble maker. Apply oil on frying pan and put the mixture by spoon. Stew until it becomes yellowish.

▶ I can make Kimchi fried rice. Cut Kimchi into suitable sizes and cut carrots and onions into 5mm lengths. Cut all beef into suitable sizes. Fry all Kimchi, garlic, and beef on a cooker and then, add the prepared onion, carrot. Finally put a little bit of salt and sesame oil.

▶ My favorite is Bibimbap. Prepare vegetables, rinse and fry. And put them on the top of steamed rice with hot chili pepper sauce and sesame oil. Hot stone bowl makes Bibimbap more delicious.

VEGETABLES		
양상추(lettuce)	양배추(cabbage)	샐러리(celery)
브로콜리(broccoli)	시금치(spinach)	가지(eggplant)
애호박(zucchini)	완두콩(pea)	오이(cucumber)
당근(carrot)	무(radish)	버섯(mushroom)
고구마(sweet potato)	피망(green pepper)	고추(red pepper)
양파(onion)	파(green onion)	강낭콩(kidney bean)

FOOD PREPARE AND RECIPE	
자르다(cut)	다지다(chop)
얇게 썰다(slice)	갈다(grind)
벗기다(peel)	젓다(stir)
기름에 볶다(saute)	붓다(pour)
얇게 썰다(carve)	굽다(bake)
삶다(boil)	튀기다(fry)
찌다(steam)	뒤섞어 익히다(scramble)
석쇠에 굽다(grill)	볶다(stir-fry)

15. What kind of TV programs do you usually watch?

🎤 국내 항공사 영어면접에서 물어볼 수 있는 질문이다. 발전적인 프로그램이나 영어 관련 프로그램을 답변하는게 효과적이다. 답변에 따라서 때로 시사문제에 대해 꼬리 질문이 나오기도 한다.

▶ I enjoy watching news, especially CNN. I need to know about current events, politics, and economics around the world.

▶ I like talk-show among Korean channels and drama series among English channels. I can experience other people's life and travel many different countries by watching those programs.

Travel / Overseas Experience

Tip

여행 경험을 이야기할 때는 육하원칙을 사용하여 간결하게 이야기하고 여행을 통해 느낀 점으로 마무리 한다. 즉, 누가(who), 언제(when), 어디서(where), 무엇을(what), 어떻게(how), 왜(why) 그리고 배운 점을 덧붙인다. 국내여행과 해외여행 한 가지씩 준비하고, 비행기를 타보았냐는 질문에는 타보았다고 하는 것이 좋다. 승무원 지망생으로서 승무원이 어떤 서비스를 하는지, 하는 일이 무엇인지 직접 보고 알고 있다는 모습을 보여주고, 여행을 간다면 어디로 가고 싶은지, 어느 나라가 가장 인상 깊었는지, 그리고 외국인에게 소개해줄 만한 우리나라 장소를 준비한다.

1. Have you ever been on board?

🎤 이 질문은 비행기를 타보았느냐는 질문이다. 가능하면 지원 항공사 탑승 경험이 있다면 좋겠다. 여행한 목적지와 Flight No.까지 알고 있다면 효과적이다.

▶ Yes, sir. I've been on KE.

2. Have you ever been abroad?

🎤 1번과 비슷할지 모르지만 이 질문은 외국에 나가본적 있냐는 질문이다. 1번 질문과 발음이 비슷하니 주의해야 한다.

▶ Yes, sir. I've been to Australia.

3. Have you ever flown in an airplane?

🎤 1번과 같은 뜻의 질문이다. 이렇게 물어볼 수도 있으니 국내 항공사 준비하는 예비지원자들은 참고하길 바란다.

▶ Yes, once on a flight from Seoul to Jeju-island.

4. Have you taken a trip recently?

🎤 이 질문은 국내여행을 답해도 무방하다. 지원하고자 하는 항공사 국내선을 타봤다고 얘기해도 좋고 여행지에 대해 소개해도 좋다.

▶ Yes, I went to Jeju-island last month.

▶ No, I haven't taken a trip for a long time.

5. What was your impression of cabin crew?

🎤 이 질문은 국내 항공사에서 나올 수 있는 질문이다. 지원하고자하는 항공사 승무원에 대해 본인이 느낀 긍정적인 점을 어필하자.

▶ They were so bright and beautiful. They worked hard and stayed focused on their duty. Their cooperation and professional attitude looked good to me. I got a good impression of them from that experience.

6. Have you ever traveled abroad? / Do you have any overseas experience?

🎤 일반적으로 여행 관련 질문에서 해외여행 경험 여부를 묻는 질문부터는 국내 항공사 / 외국 항공사 공통으로 나오고 있다. 특히 외국 항공사에서는 반드시 물어보는 질문이니 답변시 타문화에 대한 적응력을 어필하면 효과적이다.

▶ Yes, I traveled through Europe last year.

▶ No, I haven't. But I'm thinking about going to China next year.

▶ No, I haven't but I've been to many places in Korea.

▶ Yes, I've been to _____ in _____ for sightseeing (to study English).

▶ Yes, I have been to many different countries. I have been to ＿＿, ＿＿, and ＿＿. The most interesting country that I have been to is Singapore because I could see tall buildings and clean streets which are very different from those in my own country.

7. What was the most impressive traveling?

🎙 국내 항공사인 경우에는 국내여행을 얘기해도 좋지만 외국 항공사의 경우는 본인이 배운 점이 많았던 외국 여행지를 얘기해야 한다.

▶ It was my high school excursion trip. I went to Jeju-island with my high school mates for 3 overnights. We took Asiana Airlines. Cabin crews worked really hard with great smile. This island is originally volcanic island so you could see craters left. If you go there, you should not miss fresh seafood. It's the most memorable trip I've ever had.

▶ I went to China 3 years ago with friends. We went there by plane and stayed for 2 weeks. We visited many historical places and learned about Chinese customs and culture. I had a great time and I'm planning to go there again next year.

▶ My favorite traveling place was ＿＿＿＿ in ＿＿＿＿. When I went there, that place was surrounded by a beautiful nature. So, I felt like I was in heaven.

▶ ＿＿＿＿ was the most impressive place for me. I really enjoyed the time I spent there because I've always wanted to go there. Especially, I was totally over-whelmed by the beautiful night view (unforgettable sunrise / sunset) there.

8. What did you learn from that overseas experience?

🎙 다른 문화에 대한 이해, 타문화나 환경에 적응할 수 있는 능력들을 객관적으로 알 수 있는 질문이므로 짧은 기간의 여행이라도 보고 듣고 느낀 점들에 대해서 아주 긍정적으로 답변한다.

▶ I became more approachable person. At first, I was bit shy to talk with some-one who I first met but everybody say hi and talk just like friends even between strangers there. It was quite new experience for me but I really wanted to learn from them. Since I was back from there, I think I became more approachable and active than before.

▶ I became more adaptable person. Actually, it was my first time to live abroad and separate from my family. So, people and whole environment were quite new for me. From my overseas experience. I realized that I can adapt myself in any environment once I face it.

▶ I gained confidence from my experiences there. I made new friends, I adapted myself in very new environments and I solved all problems by myself while I was there. So, I became more confident in whatever I do.

▶ I became more responsible person. It was my first time to live apart from my family and I should decide everything and solve all problems by myself there. So, I felt more responsible whatever I do. So, I have become more independent and matured naturally.

▶ In order to broaden my horizons and improve English skills, I decided to leave for Sydney, Australia and stayed for about 4 months. Through these experiences, I was able to not only improve my English skills but also broaden my perspective in the world. I stayed with a local family for a month and it provided me a good chance to know about what life is like in a western country. Living alone allowed me to be more independent and responsible and I realized the importance of family.

▶ I became more approachable person through my experiences in _____. Actually, I was bit shy to talk with strangers specially foreigners. However, I tried to talk to people as much as possible, so I could feel much comfortable at the end.

▶ I became more bright person. When I went there, I realized that most of local people have smiling faces all the time. It was really impressive for me. So, I always try to have a bright face with smile in front of people through my experience there.

▶ I learned many things from my overseas experience. I participated in a film society in the US (many different activities like ~and ~). I had many chances to meet people coming from different parts of the world and went through situations that I had never experienced before. Since then, I have been able to easily get myself comfortable to new circumstances and get along well with people who are different from me.

9. What country would you like to visit in the future? / Where would you like to go if you become a cabin crew?

🎤 국내 항공사에서 자주 나오는 질문이다. 항공사 취항 노선을 잘 숙지하여 답변을 만들도록 한다.

▶ I would like to go to ___ in ____. Because, I've always wanted to see (experience / taste)_____ I will really enjoy my time if I go there. (I will make great memories if I go there.)

▶ I hope to visit Australia.

▶ I'm interested in art. So I want to visit France to see Louvre Museum.

▶ If I become a cabin crew, I would like to go to South Africa. Because I want to have a chance to see the natural environment and wildlife of the country. I've seen many pictures of the beautiful mountains and forests of South Africa. Also, I've heard Capetown described as one of the most beautiful cities in the world. I think traditional South African culture is so fascinating. There are such diverse groups living together, and I would like to learn about multi-cultural societies as well.

10. Which places would you like to recommend a foreigner who wants to go sightseeing in Korea?

🎤 서울에 대한 설명 또는 외국인들에게 소개해주고 싶은 장소에 대한 문제이다. 서울 안에서라는 단서가 주어질 경우가 있으므로 서울 안에서 한 곳을 준비하고, 그 외의 지역을 소개하고 싶은 사람은 따로 한 곳을 더 비슷한 양식으로 준비하도록 하자.

▶ I would like to recommend _____ in ___ to my foreign friend. Because, my friend can experience the true Korean culture / taste delicious korean foods / see the traditional Korean style / enjoy shopping with reasonable prices there.

▶ I've been to a lot of nice places here in Korea, but I think Jeju-island is the best. I've been there several times. It's beautiful anytime of the year.

▶ In Namsan, there are many convenient facilities for citizen. The walking and jogging course around Namsan is one of the most pleasant areas in Seoul. There is a cable car and the Seoul Tower which is a famous land mark of Seoul.

▶ I would like to recommend Bulkuksa Temple, built with a Buddhist spirit and natural surroundings, symbolizing Buddha's land on earth. Bulkuksa Temple is our great cultural heritage and I hope you could have a chance to visit Kyung-Ju.

한국의 명소 및 추천 예시

- **경주**(Gyeongju)
  - ▶ I want to recommend Gyeongju. Gyeongju city has lots of historical monuments and whole street antic and traditional atmosphere. People of Gyeongju are kind. If you look around the whole city by cycling, it will be more exciting.

- **부산**(Busan)
  - ▶ I want to recommend Busan. Busan is well known for beautiful beaches and various fish market. Especially the magnificent night view of Kwang-an bridge is my favorite. In there you can taste fresh seafood and raw fish while having the whole view of sea.
  - ▶ I want to suggest you to visit Busan. It's on the southern edge of Korea. There you can enjoy the seaside and delicious seafood as well. If you can wake up early, you can see the sunrise from horizon.

- **서울 – 인사동/청계천**
  - ▶ I want to recommend Insa-dong. It is traditional street where you can spend buying souvenirs and tasting traditional cuisines of Korea Especially on Sundays, cars are not allowed, so you can take a walk experiencing various Korea sightseeing. I recommend you to visit there on Sunday.
  - ▶ Insa-dong is famous place in Seoul. There are many Korean traditional souvenirs and also can enjoy various street performances and art galleries. You can taste delicious cuisine and traditional tea on an antic and cozy style restaurant which are located at Insa-dong area.
  - ▶ I recommend you Insa-dong. You are able to see co-exciting image of past and present of Korea. In there, you can experience traditional Korean culture and visit lots of traditional Tea House. This area has become one of the most famous tourist attractions for foreigners.
  - ▶ I want to recommend Cheonggyecheon Stream. In between modernized high skyscrapers, you can feel fresh and clean beauty of nature. During winter time you can enjoy the lighting show of luminaires. Many people go there to have relaxing time.

- **제주도**(Jeju-island)

  ▶ I want to recommend Jeju-island. Jeju is famous for three manies - lady, rocks and winds. This island is originally volcanic island so you could see craters left. If you go there, you should not miss fresh seafood and beautiful nature.

 서울의 명소 소개 예시

- **한옥마을**(Hanok Village)

  ▶ It was used for Korean upper class' village. Traditional style of houses and garden will make you feel comfortable like your home. Also they have had time capsule to show you history and celebration for 600 years as the capital city of Korea.

- **롯데월드**(Lotte World Theme Park)

  ▶ This huge shopping and entertainment complex offers visitors the chance to experience a folk village, adventure and sports center as well as hotel and department store. One of the major reasons tourists are attracted to Lotte World is the amusement rides. You will have new kinds of fun through the Lotte World.

- **한강유람선**(Han River Cruise)

  ▶ A boat cruise along the Han River is one of the best way to enjoy the scenery of Seoul city. In particular, the ferry cruise can offer you the beautiful and romantic scenery in the evening.

- **월드컵 경기장**(World Cup Stadium)

  ▶ Seoul World Cup Stadium is shaped like a traditional Korean kite and seen from above, it looks as if a rectangular shield is being flown like a kite. It acco- modates about 60,000 seats. The area and facility of this stadium is the best in Asia.

외국 항공사 추가질문 − Emotion−Related Questions

1. What was the most difficult thing when you stay there?

🎙 이는 여행 관련 질문에서 핵심이 되는 질문이다. 어려운 점을 해결하면서 더욱 독립적이고 자신감을 키웠던 경험으로 이야기를 풀어나간다.

▶ The most difficult thing was to get used to their pronunciation and speed when I talk with people. I didn't have much time to talk with foreigners in Korea. So, when I talk to people, they speak too fast and even pronunciation was not easy for me. Of course, I went there to study English so I was a beginner but still it was bit difficult and stressful sometimes.

▶ The most difficult thing was to adapt myself in totally different environment. Actually, it was the first time to experience all surroundings were changed including language, people and place. Of course, I went there to study and experience those new things but still it was a really big change so quite difficult at first.

▶ The most difficult thing was weather. It was too hot and humid compare with summer in Korea, so I felt quite difficult to walk around outside. However, I thought it's the part of traveling, so I could stand it.

▶ The most difficult thing was the food. Most of the foods were too oily and greasy for me. However, I tried to enjoy those foods with the local people and their atmosphere. So, I could slowly overcome that difficultiy.

▶ It was not easy to adapt myself in totally new environment. I thought the best way to adapt myself there is to go out with active attitude and meet people, So I started meeting a lot of local people. So I get used to those new surroundings by getting useful local informations from them.

▶ Well, there wasn't any difficulty for me in Sydney. In fact, it was very interesting and exciting learning there culture. The only inconvenient thing was that I didn't have a car so it was hard to go around. Other than that, I really loved living in Sydney.

▶ When I was traveling in Japan I sometimes had trouble communicating. I can only speak English and Korean. They didn't understand my English and I could not understand Japanese. It was a little inconvenient because of the language barrier. But I tried hard to make myself understood using gestures and body language and it worked. From this I felt more comfortable interacting with people who speak different languages.

▶ Paying for tuition and living expenses was my responsibility when I study in Sydney. To do that, I had to work on a farm for 6months and it was not easy job to do. But I worked hard and managed to stay in Sydney as I planned. From this I got sense of achievement and became more confident in my ability to deal with any situation.

2. What was a cultural difference you experienced there?

🎤 개개인의 경험에서 온 일화나 작은 문화적 차이를 얘기한다. 다른 나라의 문화를 비방해선 안된다. 다른 것이 틀린 것은 아님을 명심하자. 또한 낯선 환경에서의 자신의 적응력을 부각시키자. 낯선 환경에서 잘 적응하고 성과를 이루었다는 것을 보여주는 것이 포인트이다.

▶ It seemed like they act more natural way even in front of others. In Korea, we usually really care about others and how I look, so we tend to be more careful about behaviour and dress code. However, I saw many people singing on the street and lay down anywhere and talk to each other. Also, they wear very casual clothes even for classes or when they hanging out. That was quite different from Koreans.

▶ It was amazing that nobody asked my age there. In Korea, when we meet new people we ask their name and age first but they think it's kind of personal. Also, we all can be just friends regardless of age. It was quite new and interesting for me.

▶ It seemed great that people always take time and hardly ever in hurry. We usually walk fast and do things very quickly in Korea, so I felt things and even people are quite slow there but I found it's really great they never in hurry and relaxed.

3. What do you think about the differences between Korean and Western people?

🎤 주로 유럽 항공사 쪽에서 많이 나온다. 두 문화의 다른점을 이야기 하는것이지 어느 한 문화가 부정적으로 비춰지면 안된다. 문화에 대한 이해, 극복 방법이 중요하기 때문이다. 다르다고 틀린것은 아니다. 유럽항공사에서 한국인 승무원을 채용하는 이유는 한국인 승객을 위해서이기도 하다.

▶ I think we, Koreans sometimes care too much of what other people say or think of us. So Koreans seem to pay much attention to other people's views. On the other hand, Western people don't seem to care much about what other people think about them. I think Western people are more relaxed about themselves.

4. Have you experienced any culture shock?

🎤 앞서 언급했듯이 답변 시 다른 문화를 비하하는 발언이나 무시하는 내용은 삼가 하여야 한다. 다만 한국과 다른것들을 객관적으로 풀어나가야 한다. 특히 일본이나 중국의 경우 따라오는 꼬리 질문은 그 나라 사람들에 대한 것 또는 한국과 다른 점 등을 물어볼 수 있다. 특별한 것이 없었을 경우 아래와 같이 답한 후 자연스럽게 간단한 문화차이에 대한 답변으로 넘어갈 수 있다.

▶ Well, there was no special culture shock for me living in other country, In fact, it was very interesting and exciting to meet variety of people. And, learning the culture was such a wonderful experience for me.

▶ I thought their culture was not much different from ours. But the one thing that surprised me was that when I stayed in the countryside in China they didn't have doors in the public toilets. I was a little embarrassed when I first saw them. But I thought it was just part of the culture.

5. How did you adapt yourself in new environment?

🎤 적응력을 물어보는 질문이다. 당연히 잘 적응을 한다고 답변을 해야하며 그랬던 예를 꼭 부연설명으로 넣도록 하자.

▶ As I mentioned, I went there to experience new things so I kept telling myself I can adjust to new situation there with my positive attitude and in time things got easier. Everyone would feel the same if they were in my situation, so I didn't take those difficulties too seriously and I made many different friends by going to parties and being involved in activities to feel familiar with my new surroundings.

6. How do you approach people(How do you make friends)?

🎤 여기에서 외국 항공사의 경우 따라오는 꼬리 질문은 '그래서 어떤 이야기를 했는가?'이다.
간단히 그 나라말 인사말 배우기, 그 나라의 유명한 곳에 대해 묻기, 그 나라의 기본적인 사항이나 음식에 대해서 묻기 등 각 나라별로 준비해 두면 좋다.

▶ I try to say hi first. At the beginning, I am a bit shy to do so but I felt I can not make many friends if I always wait for them to come to me and say hi. Once we start a conversation with saying hi, then I show my interest about their country, famous sightseeing places, and language. There is no one who hates to answer when someone is interested in their own country. I also feel happy when people ask me about Korea.

7. How will you live apart from your family? / How would you like to adapt yourself in other country?

🎤 이는 주로 외국에 거점을 두고 있는 항공사들이 채용 시 적응력을 판별하기 위하여 주로 사용하는 질문이다. 외국 항공사 지원자들은 자신이 적응력, 독립심이 있다는 것을 보여주기 위해 적절한 본인의 경험담을 준비해 두는 것이 좋다.

▶ Family means a lot to me so I will miss them of course. However, it will be a great chance for me to be more independent and to challenge myself with various experiences, so I will keep convincing myself I'm strong enough to overcome loneliness. Also, I can make close friends and release my feelings by talking and enjoying time with them because usually when we talk about something we feel much more comfortable.

7

School Life

 Tip

학교생활에서 중요한 문제는 전공에 대한 전문성과 동아리 활동 경험이다. 최근에는 자원봉사 경험과 아르바이트 경험 등 폭 넓은 영역으로 질문이 나오므로 준비하도록 한다.

[학사] B.A.=Bachelor of Arts(학사:문과) B.S.=Bachelor of Science(학사:이과)

[석사] M.A.=Master of Arts(석사:문과)   M.S.=Master of Science(석사:이과)

1. Which university do you attend?

▶ I attend Korea University.

▶ I attend (am graduated from) 000 Univ (college). It is located in _____, next to (near) _____. (외국인 면접관이 잘 모르는 지역일 수 있으므로 유명한 도시 어디 근처인지 언급할 것) It is famous for _____.(특정 학과, 스포츠 팀, 종합병원, 동문의 유명인 등) (특정 유명한 것이 없을 시는 아래와 같이 답하면 된다.) It is famous for a beautiful campus. Also, It is famous for various language exchange programs with university in _____ and _____. (중국, 일본, 미국 등의 학교와 자매결연, 교환학생 프로그램이 있는 경우 이를 이야기 하는 것도 좋다.)

2. What year are you in?

🎤 국내 항공사에서 의외로 이 질문을 못알아 듣는 지원자가 있다. 현재 몇학년이냐는 질문이므로 각 학년의 표현법을 익히도록 한다.

▶ I'm a freshman / sophomore / junior / senior.

▶ I'm a freshman studying medicine at Korea University.

3. What's your major? / What are you majoring in? / What are you studying?

🎤 전공에 대한 질문은 국내 항공사에서 많이 나오고 또 외국 항공사에서는 스크리닝 인터뷰때 나오기도 한다. 서비스직과 관련이 없는 전공이라도 분명 배운 점은 많다. 그러므로 자신감을 가지고 전공을 어필하도록 한다.

▶ My major is English.

▶ I'm majoring in chemistry.

▶ I majored in Tourism, English literature, Economics, History in University.

▶ My major is _____. I learned the basic knowledge of _____ and _____. It was not easy (bit difficult) but really useful / informative and interesting / practical study for me.

4. What was your favorite course?

🎤 국내 항공사에서만 물어볼 수 있다. 서비스 직종과 관련이 없는 전공이라도 어학을 얘기할 수 있으며 찾아보면 도움이 되는 과목들이 있으므로 잘 어필하도록 하자.

▶ My favorite course was English. I studied really hard and tried to make foreign friends. I went to Sydney to study English about 6 months and that experience was useful.

5. Why did you choose this as your major?

🎤 전공이 이공계 혹은 특이한 경우 물어볼 수 있다. 중요한 점은 나의 전공에 대해 자부심을 갖고 긍정적으로 이야기해야 한다는 것이다.

▶ I was interested in _____ field when I was a high school student. And I though it was related with real life and helpful for me.

6. Do you have any licenses or certificates?

🎤 국내 항공사에서 자격증에 대해 물을때 이처럼 묻기도 한다. 승무원 관련 수료증은 여러 가지가 있을 수 있겠다. 작은 경험이라도 모두 다 얘기하도록 한다.

▶ Yes, I have studied English to be an English tour guide for about 3 years, and I have passed the English tour guide exam three months ago and finished a training course for tour guide last week.

7. Could you introduce your major?

🎤 일반적으로 '전공이 무엇이야'라고 물을 수 있지만 이처럼 '전공을 소개해 달라'고 할 수도 있다. 이 질문에는 전공을 통해 배운 점까지 이야기 하도록 한다.

▶ My major is _____. I learned the basic knowledge of _____ and _____. It was not easy but really useful / informative / interesting for me. Specially, it was great to feel more familiarized with _____ through various classes.

▶ I majored in Tourism management. I studied about basic understanding of the fundamentals in the tourism and how to manage hotel, travel agency, restaurant, and so on. My graduation thesis was the history of Korea tourism.

8. What was the most impressive thing during your school days?

🎤 이 또한 국내, 외항사 모두 나올 수 있다. 학교생활 중에 가장 큰 업적, 성과 등을 어필하도록 한다. 이러한 큰 성과물이 면접관으로 하여금 승무직에 적합한 인재라는 인상을 줄 수 있는 에피소드가 효과적이다.

▶ The most impressive thing was my club activities / volunteering works / travel experience to _____. I went to 여행 도시 for 여행 혹은 연수 기간 to study / for sightseeing. I participated in volunteer works to help _____. I really had a great time there.

▶ I always reviewed what I had learned and previewed the subjects I would study. And I still do. And I resulted in getting all A+ and got a scholarship at the end of the second semester. This is one of my greatest achievements.

9. Were you ever involved in any activities during your school days?

🎤 학창시절 기억에 남는 일에 여행 또는 동아리 활동을 말하고 이 활동을 통해 학교 공부 이외의 leadership, friendship, responsibility 등의 가치 있는 것들을 배울 수 있었다고 한다.

▶ Yes, sir. I participated in _____ club. We practiced every Friday after school and once a semester we performed on the stage. I learned the teamwork and how to take care of others.

▶ I joined the volunteer work club. We often visited children's house and old people's house. I came to realize that it's very important to help poor people.

10. What is the relation between your major and the job of cabin crew?

🎤 국내 항공사에서 압박질문의 형태로 나올 수 있는 질문이다. 명심할 것은 어떤 전공이라도 배운 점은 분명히 있으며 찾기가 힘들다면 연결이 될 수 있는 실마리를 찾아 이야기 하도록 한다. 예를 들면 교과목 중에는 어학, 국제문화, 커뮤니케이션 등 분명 승무원으로서 필요한 과목을 배운적이 있을 것이다. 그때 흥미로웠던 경험을 이야기해도 된다는 것이다.

▶ I've been studying about hotel, travel and management. So I guess I can understand traveler's mind very well and treat them comfortably with my travel knowledge. I truly believe that my experience and knowledge I have learned through undergraduate and graduate years will be a valuable asset to your company.

▶ My major is food and nutrition. I've been studying about food for healthy life. If I become a cabin crew, I'd like to recommend suitable food for children, old people, and people with allergy.

▶ I understand it seems like there is no connection between my major and this job. However, I believe my major would be helpful because I learned about _____. It allow me to learn / have / understand _____.

11. How was your school life?

🎙 이는 전반적인 학교생활이 어땠는지에 대한 질문이다. 국내, 외항 모두 자주 물어보는 질문이다. 성적이 좋다면 수업, 그 외 서비스직 아르바이트 경험, 봉사활동, 자격증, 팀프로젝트 등등 전반적으로 다 포함 되도록 한다.

▶ It was great. I enjoyed my major so I had a good GPA and got scholarships during my university days. It was really meaningful time for me.

▶ It was great. I was a member of a student association, so I've done various activities during university major events. It was really meaningful time for me.

▶ It was great. I was a member of _____ club, so I had many performances / attended festival /enjoyed _____ with club members / had a great time with our club members. It was really meaningful time for me.

▶ It was really instructive and interesting. I had almost perfect attendance record. I studied my major as well as cultural subjects. I was happy I could meet various friends from different cities. The greatest thing was that everybody treated me as an adult.

12. What did you learn from your club activities?

🎙 이는 국내 항공사에서 물어볼 수 있는 질문이다. 동아리 활동에 대해 묻는 질문이다. 팀웍, 자신감 등등 향상된 점을 긍정적으로 어필하도록 한다.

▶ I became more approachable person through my club activities. I met various people at club, so I had many chances to talk with new faces. So, it became much easier to start conversation with anyone.

▶ I became more energetic person through my club activities. We had same taste for enjoying _____, so it was always so energetic and fun when we were together. So, I became more passionate and active now.

13. What did you learn from your volunteer work?

🎙 갈수록 자원봉사 경력에 대한 중요성이 높아지고 있다. 외항사를 지원하는 경우 면접관이 공감할 만한 외국 봉사활동 경험을 얘기할 수 있다면 훨씬 좋은 인상을 줄 수 있다.

▶ I've done volunteer works at _____. I thought I've done something special for those people at the beginning, but I learned much more valuable things from them at the end.

14. Who was your favorite teacher in high school?

🎤 선생님을 존경하는 이유, 배우고 싶은 점에 관련된 질문들은 국내 항공사에서 가끔 나오기도 한다.

▶ My favorite teacher was ____. He was a chemistry teacher. He was very funny and pleasant person. He always tried to make the class interesting and he treated a person with consideration. And he explained about difficult question over and over until we understand about that. I'd like to meet him again someday.

▶ I respect my high school teacher. He had so much humors and vitalities, and he was a man of discretion very much. He could make a person see the mistakes without making him feel foolish. I learned a lot from watching the way he applied himself to his teaching, and how he led people to see things.

15. How did you study English?

🎤 이 질문은 국내 항공사뿐 아니라 의외로 외국 항공사에서도 많이 물어본다. 영어 공부를 하는 것이 비단 학원을 다닌다고 하는 것보다 스스로, 그리고 함께 꾸준히 한다는 인상을 주면 효과적이다.

▶ I thought the best way to learn language is to listen and memorize and use it. So, whenever I talk to my foreign friends (watch English drama / movies / tapes), I listen carefully and try to memorize their expressions and use them when I talk. It was really helpful to improve my English.

▶ I was not fluent in English but I thought if I don't actively use it, then there's no way to learn that. So, I tried keep talking even I made some mistakes and tried to minimize those mistakes afterwards. That's how I could improve my English in a short period of time. (faster than other classmates there)

Job Experiences

Tip

재학시절 했던 아르바이트나 자원봉사의 경험, 졸업 후 했던 일에 대한 질문이다. 특히 아르바이트는
서비스와 관련된 것이면 더 좋다. 이 파트의 질문 모두 국내 항공사와 외국 항공사 모두 나오는 문제
들이므로 아주 중요하다. 일 경험의 질문은 이력서 또는 지원서 바탕으로 물어보기 때문에 단기간의
아르바이트의 경우라도 꼼꼼하게 작성하도록 한다. 학생이라도 지원서의 일 경험을 공란으로 내게 되
면 1차에서 불합격할 수 있으니 꼭 기억하자.

1. Did you have part time experience during school days?
/ Have you ever worked? / Do you have any part time
experience(work experience)? / What have you been doing since
graduating from college?

🎤 '언제, 어디서, 얼마동안, 어떤 일을 했는가, 일을 통해 느낀 점은 무엇인가' 의 구조로 답변하
도록 한다.

▶ Yes, I have. I worked at _____ as a _____ (waitress / sales clerk / assistant) for
_____ months.

▶ Yes, I worked at a coffee shop as a waitress and book store as a receptionist
during each vacation. So I could help for my tuition.

▶ Yes, when I was in university, I used to work as a sales clerk in a department store.

▶ I had a part time job at OO hotel during my winter vacation. And I worked at a cafe as a waitress for the last 6 months. I enjoyed meeting a lot of people and through these experiences I realized how important human relationships are.

▶ Yes, I had a part time job at TGI restaurant as a waitress for 3 months.

▶ Yes, I volunteered at _____ rehabilitation center for children as a teacher assistant and I cooked, cleaned and played with children.

▶ I have worked for OO department store as a sales clerk for three years. Since I resigned last year, I have been attending an English conversation class at a private institute, where Americans teach.

2. Which company do you work for?

🎤 현재 재직 중인 경우 본인이 하고 있는 일에 대한 정확한 설명이 필요하다.

▶ I work for ___company.

▶ I'm an employee of the ____ company.

3. How long have you been working there?

🎤 얼마동안 일했느냐는 질문이다. 현재도 일하고 있다면 아래와 같이, 이미 그만뒀다면 과거형으로 표현하자.

▶ I've been working there for about 2 years.

4. What made you decide to switch positions?

🎤 이 질문은 이직 경험이 있는 지원자에게 해당되는 질문이다. 명심해야 하는건 어떤 이유라도 전직장을 비하하거나 힘들다는 표현은 금물이다.

▶ I have several reasons. I like to meet various kinds of people and travel. And I would like to get a job which I can use English.

▶ I want to work in a continually changing, active and cheerful job atmosphere so that I can enjoy my work.

5. Do you prefer working alone or with others?

🎤 이 질문은 가끔 국내 항공사에서 나온다. 승무원이라면 둘 다 가능해야 한다. 균형을 맞추되 더 좋은것을 얘기해도 된다.

▶ I'm good at working in a group as well as working by myself. I prefer working with others who have more experience than me because I can learn from the team members. I also like working alone because I can stay more focused and because I don't need to pay attention to other things such as setting a meeting date and working on relations with other team members.

6. How do you define 'leadership'?

🎤 의외로 이 질문은 국내 항공사에서 나온다. 간혹 외국 항공사의 경우는 지원자가 리더의 자질에 대해 이야기를 꺼낸다면 따라올 수 있는 꼬리질문이다.

▶ I would define leadership as establishing a common goal and motivating people to achieve it. A good leader is someone who has positive energy and uses their intelligence to teach and guide others. They are natural motivators and listen well and talk openly with team members.

7. What did you learn or gain from your past experience (part-time / internship)?

🎤 일경험 중 핵심이 되는 질문이라고 하겠다. 외국 항공사의 경우는 본인의 경험담도 이야기하도록 한다.

▶ I have learned many things from my various activities in and out of school. First, I have learned to organize my work. Whenever I am given tasks, I always prioritize them first. Second, I have acquired team oriented attitude through many team projects. Last, I have learned good interpersonal skills through many extracurricular activities.

▶ From my job experience I learned some lessons. I learned that the results from hard work are always pleasant, Earning money is not easy, but there is a bigger society waiting for me.

▶ I learned how much important team work and patience are.

▶ The most significant thing that I have learned is understand other's mind.

▶ I learned how to communicate effectively and constructively.

▶ I learned that being professional and keeping a good attitude was important in order to take care of customers properly.

▶ I became more responsible person. In the work place, there are my own part and task. If I'm not fully in charge of them, I could ruin whole team work. That's why I learned I should always complete my duties with responsibility.

▶ I became more patient person. When I worked there, I had quite long working hours. Also, I had to get though many difficulties. That's why I could learned the true meaning of patience.

▶ I learned the importance of team work. When I worked there, I couldn't make all the customers happy by myself. I could make them satisfied and achieve a good results only through great team work with my co-workers.

▶ I worked as a OOOO, I learned what is so-called tailored service. Because I became aware that every single customer had its own preference.

8. Can you work under pressure?

🎤 이는 앞에도 언급되었던 질문이지만 조금 다른 점은 그런 환경에서 일을 할 수 있겠는가이다. 당연히 답변은 그렇다고 얘기한 후 경험담을 이야기하도록 한다.

▶ Many people think stress is bad, but it is said that a certain amount of stress motivates us to do our jobs better. Even when I get stressed out, I try to stay calm. I don't get angry or upset easily, because I approach it logically. I always tend to be cautious when I make any decisions. When I have problems I approach them logically not emotionally.

9. What was the most difficult thing when you work there?

🎙 이 또한 배운 점과 함께 핵심이 되는 질문이다. 외항사에서 자주 물어본다. 힘들었지만 극복 방법도 얘기하고 그런 경험을 통해 결과적으로 배운 점까지 어필할 수 있는 좋은 질문이라고 하겠다.

▶ I had pain in my legs and sometimes customers complained for no reason. But I kept on massaging my legs and whenever I was in trouble with customers or colleagues, I solved it out with wisdom and wits through communication.

▶ The most difficult problem I had was explaining company policy to people. I had to explain firmly but gently to prevent complaint.

▶ Sometimes customer complaints about something and I have to solve it out. Whenever I handle this kind of difficult customer, I feel so in despair. But I tried to refresh my mind and did my best for the rest of customers.

▶ Customers have all different preferences, so it was not easy for me to catch them and offer the right service to each of them. So, I watched their behaviors and I listened carefully to catch their demands.

▶ When I deal with customers, I should always have a smiling face. I understand it is a part of my duty but sometimes it could be stressful, specially when I'm sick or in a bad mood due to hear bad news. However, I did my best to control my mind and smile in front of customers.

▶ I couldn't treat them in the same way I did to others. So I had to try to be vigilant and listen more carefully to figure out what they wanted from me.

▶ It was not easy to work as a team with many team members having all different styles (different opinions). Everyone insisted their own ideas, so I suggested to do kind of a secret vote which was all of members write down the second best idea from other's opinion except their own ideas. I thought it's fair to everyone and people accept it.

9

Teamwork / Co-worker Relationship

 Tip

팀워크는 면접에서 가장 중요한 부분이다. 모든 승무원은 팀으로 일한다. 그러므로 다른 동료와도 화합하며 잘 지낼 수 있다는 긍정적인 답변이 필요하다. 이 부분에서 어필을 잘 하면 면접에서 성공할 가능성이 커진다.

1. Have you worked in a team? / Do you have team work experience?

🎤 이 질문에 대해 답변을 할 때에는 팀웍으로 일하는게 아주 좋았다라는 긍정적인 답변을 함께 해주면 효과적이다.

▶ Yes, I have. During my university days I participated as a member of ○○○club and many volunteer activities. I think I am a good team player.

▶ Yes, In my university, I've worked on several team projects, serving as both a member and team leader. I've seen the value of working together as a team to achieve a greater goal than any one of us could have achieved individually.

▶ Yes, I'm working at an family restaurant as a waitress and there are about 7 co-workers I work with. During lunch or dinner time, it can be very busy so we try to communicate each other and work well to serve the customers smoothly.

2. What did you learn from team activities?

🎙 이는 보통 1번 질문 다음에 나올 수 있는 꼬리질문이다. 2번에서 언급한 가이드라인을 따라 답변을 만들도록 한다.

▶ I learned a lot from my team project. My manager taught us that the most important part was waiting out for others. She said that if you do that, you will always have someone waiting for you as well. It is exactly the strategy that I have tried to apply to my daily life.

3. What do you think is the most important thing when you work in a team?

🎙 팀으로 일을 할 때에는 커뮤니케이션 스킬, 상대방에 대한 배려심 등등 각자가 중요하게 생각하는 부분을 강조하면 된다. 외항사 면접 시 꼬리 질문으로 '좋은 팀웍을 이뤘던 예'를 들라고도 할 수 있으니 외항사 지원자들은 본인의 경험담을 함께 준비하도록 한다.

▶ I consider communication is one of the most important things in working as a team. We have the same goal to accomplish in a team. I think communication and sharing information can bring people together and makes people work more efficiently.

▶ I believe there are so many things but I could say being cooperative and responsible are important things in working with other people in a team. We should work together to support each other on the mission assigned.

4. What was the most difficult thing when you worked as a team?

🎙 팀으로 일할 때 배운 점과 힘든 점은 중요한 질문들이다. 하지만 극복 방법과 그로 인해 지금은 어떻게 달라졌는지 어필하는 것을 잊지말자.

▶ Well, I like working as a team but sometimes it is difficult to cooperate with others when we have to make a decision without enough time left. When I worked at my previous company, we had only few hours to decide and each of us had our own preference. There was not enough time to respect every individual's opinion but, through lively discussions, finally we decided. Obviously, there were a few who didn't like the idea but I and people who had the same opinion tried to persuade them to accept the decision as a whole. At that time, I realized that it is not easy at all to work with others cooperatively.

외국 항공사 추가질문 – Emotion-Related Questions

1. What type of co-worker do you feel uncomfortable to work with?

🎙 어떤 타입의 동료가 일하기 불편하냐는 질문은 답변 시 유의해야 할 점이 있다. 상대 동료는 나와 다를 뿐 틀리다고 지적하면 안된다.

❶ I understand that I can not choose co-workers to work with and I am willing to work with anyone. However it won't be pleasant if someone is negative about everything. But as a team I should work well with any co-worker.

• How will you work with her / him?

🎙 꼬리질문으로 본인의 people skill을 보여줘야 하는 부분이다. 어떤 경우에도 공감과 도와주는 마음가짐이 필수일 것이다.

▶ I think sometimes she just needs someone to just listen carefully and understand her. I might listen to her even though I don't have any feed-back to solve the situation. Also I will try to spread my positive energy to my co-worker because I have plenty of it.

❷ Well, I can work well with any type of co-workers. However, if someone avoids responsibility, I think it might slow down the work, which is not very effective, especially when the working time is limited.

❸ I am willing to work harder to help her job and speed up my work be-cause I know that I have passengers to serve and jobs to finish. How-ever, I would ask her to work with me when I am not able to handle by myself.

2. Have you ever got any feedback from your boss?

🎙 이 질문은 상사뿐 아니라 senior도 해당된다. 또한 피드백을 통해 지금은 어떻게 달라졌는지, 그 당시에 어떤 노력을 했는지도 어필한다.

▶ When I worked as a waitress in Australia, I got feedback from my boss that I treated customers so formally that I made them uncomfortable. Since it is kind of family restaurant, he said that I needed to be a little bit more casual when I served them. But I was not familiar with serving and I was afraid that I would make a mistake. As time passed and I learned from other servers, I got to know how to serve customers comfortably as my boss had asked me to. It was the first time for me to work in foreign country and I still think it was one of valuable experiences.

3. Have you got any good feedback or compliments from your work place?

🎙 좋은 피드백 / 칭찬을 받은 경험을 묻는 질문이다. 두 가지 중 어떤 형식으로 질문이 나와도 같은 뜻이다.

▶ Yes, I have. When I worked as a waitress in Australia, I got a lot of complement from my co-workers. They liked my smile and Korean style courtesy. When elderly customers came in, I treated them like my grandma or talked with them like a friend, helped them eat and took care of them kindly. My coworkers were impressed by my consideration for customers.

▶ I learned this in Korea by working with co-workers. When I had worked as a part-timer in Korea, I got positive feedback from my boss that I was good at dealing with customers and he said that I could work well in the service field.

4. Have you made your co-worker disappointed?

🎙 동료를 실망시켰던 경험, 나아가 화나게 했던 경험(둘 다 비슷한 종류의 질문이다.)에서는 의도치 않게 그랬던 경험, 그리고 그로 인해 그 동료를 위해 어떤 노력을 했는지, 관계가 어땠는지도 답변에 넣도록 한다.

▶ Well, most of time, I gave my co-workers a positive impression and tried to make them feel proud of me. Once, However, I disappointed my senior. I worked as a waitress and most of my co-workers from different countries. Then one day, I became a friend with a co-worker who just came from Korea and she helped me updated news about Korea. By that time, I missed Korea so much. So we talked a lot in Korean. At that time, my senior told me that it was not nice to speak in Korean since they were other people who didn't understand Korean. It was rude but I didn't realize at that time. I apologized for that I disappointed her and never did that again.

5. Have you said "No" to your coworker?

🎙 질문에서 'No'라고 묻는 의도를 파악해야 한다. 명심할 것은 어떤 경우라고 면접관의 공감을 이끌어내야 할 것이다. 사소한 에피소드를 얘기한다면 자칫 예민하거나 속 좁은 사람으로 비춰질 수 있다.

▶ It was when I worked as a manager at a restaurant. On Friday evening, the hall was crowded and they were so many on the waiting list as well. One of my co-worker came up to me to say that her family would come soon and asked me if they could get a table first. We had a long line of customer waiting to be seated at that time and I told her that I couldn't do that. I said it was not fare to other customers and I wouldn't do that even for my family. I continued to say in addition, if they had known about this, it would have hurt reputation of the restaurant. It was not easy to say "No" to my co-worker, but I was sure that I was doing right thing and she accepted it as well.

6. Have you had any conflict with your co-worker?

🎙 자신의 interpersonal skill과 problem solving skill을 어필할 수 있다. 거의 모든 외국 항공사 면접에서 나오는 질문이므로 반드시 준비를 하도록 하자.

▶ Most of time, I had a good relationship with my co-workers. But I remember one time I had a little trouble with one who was often late. At first, she seemed to be really sorry for being late and I could feel that. I took her duty without saying anything. Because we all could be late sometimes and when I am late, I thought, she could do the same for me. So, I just let it go. But she didn't change her habit and worse yet she didn't feel sorry for coming late anymore. When she was not there on time, I had my work doubled. She seemed to be not aware of that so I had to kindly tell her not to be late. She was not offended and understood me. So she apologized and we could continue to work together without any trouble.

▶ When I have a problem with my co worker (my boss) I remind that we are all different and difference is not wrong. We are from different backgrounds so we think and act different way. Once I talk about any problem, I keep that in my mind and listen what they want to say to me and tell them how I feel. I cannot solve all problems only with this but it really helps to think this way.

▶ Whenever I have a problem with someone during work, I remind the fact that I'm basically there to work. Some people are too much obsessed with uncomfortable relationship or little problems even when they work but it is bigger problem then trouble or conflict itself. So, I focus on my duty first and then if I have time then I talk and solve the problem. That's my principle.

▶ I try to convince myself conflict or disagreement is something could be happened naturally because we are all quite different each other. Which means, I still have a conversation and try to solve the problem but I don't try to fix or change them. I try to accept them as they are. It's not actually for them. It's for me and reduce my own stress.

7. Have you suggested any creative opinion to your co-worker?

🎤 팀으로 일하면서 일의 효율성 등을 위해 작은 부분이라도 창의적인 제안을 해서 성과가 좋았던 경험을 이야기한다.

▶ It was when I worked as a waitress at the restaurant. It was a national holiday and there were not many customers so just four of us worked that day. It was not that busy in the morning but suddenly a group of people came in. They were more than 20 and we got extremely busy because they were just half of staffs normally working. We devided in two teams. One rearranged tables, another took orders and served them. And I thought that if we took orders of 20 different dishes, chefs could not deal with orders all at once. So I suggested we could make simple menu with one style of steak, pizza, pasta and salad on it. Then they could enjoy what they wanted to have and chefs could make food quikly. My boss agreed with me and explained the situation to the customers and everything worked well.

Service / Customer

 Tip

서비스 분야에서 한 번도 근무한 적이 없다 하더라도 좋은 서비스가 무엇인지 반드시 인지하고 있어야 한다. 또한 내가 생각하는 서비스 정의가 있다면 '그러한 서비스를 제공하거나 받은 적이 있는지'에 대한 질문에도 일관성 있게 답변해야 할 것이다.

1. What do you think of good service? / Could you define good service?

▶ In my opinion, good service is giving full satisfaction to customers and taking care of them the best way I possibly can. If I'm hired, I will do everything in my power to make customer happy with my service, of course, while still staying in the company's guidelines.

▶ I understand that good service is treating customers with a polite and helpful attitude. It means that I should always be polite, attentive and help my customer as much as I can. If I work as cabin crew in your airline, I will always be working with this attitude even on my worst days.

▶ My basic rule of good service is to treat customers the way I want to be treated. When I worked in the service industry, I always treated my customers with courtesy and respect. If I work as cabin crew in your airline, I will always make sure that passengers leave an aircraft feeling satisfied with my service.

▶ I think good service is doing my best to make sure customers happy. When customers are happy they remember the service. I believe happy customers will provide repeat business. Also they will always be willing to recommend my company and mention it to his or her friends to come and experience it.

▶ I think good service means customer satisfaction and exceeding customers' expectations. I understand that every customer expects a certain amount of service, some more than others. It would be great if I hear them saying, "Wow, I didn't expect that" or 'Thank you very much, You are very kind." Then they are more likely to remember me and come back to use our service.

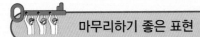

마무리하기 좋은 표현

- If I work as cabin crew in your airline, I will always make sure that I give the best service to each customer.

- I will always treat my customers with a friendly and helpful attitude. (with a bright smile and respect).

2. When was the time you made your customer very satisfied and happy with your service? / Have you helped your customer in special way?

🎤 고객을 만족시켰던 경험 / 도와줬던 경험 등은 비슷한 답변으로 준비해도 된다. 자신이 생각하는 좋은 서비스 정의와 일관성 있는 답변이 좋다.

▶ Most recently when I was working for fast food restaurant as a part timer, I always tried to be helpful to my customers. Sometimes I had a customer come into the store and they didn't exactly know what they wanted, especially the elderly customers. So I explained about each item on the menu which they might like and the special set menu so that they could take advantage of the discounts. They said I was very kind and helpful to them. It felt great when customers appreciated my service.

▶ Currently I am working as a sales assistant in a bakery. My duties normally are wrapping baked goods, handling cash and keeping the area neat and clean. However, when a customer has a lot to carry I willingly help them with a smile to carry their bags to their car or taxi stand. They are always happy with my help and most of them are coming back to the shop.

3. What kind service would you offer to your passengers if you work as a cabin crew?

🎤 이는 국내 항공사에서 주로 물어 보는 질문이다. 이 또한 지원자의 서비스에 대한 기본적인 생각을 알 수 있는 질문이므로 앞서 나왔던 '좋은 서비스'에 대한 정의와 연관성있게 준비하도록 한다.

▶ I will always respond to my passengers in a friendly and professional manner. I will also provide what they need without any delay and satisfy their expectations with a bright smile and kindness. I will absolutely ensure that I give the best service to each customer.

▶ I fully understand that I am not only the face and the representative of myself but also the company while I wear the uniform. I will definitely try all I can do to give good impression to my passengers so that they will fly with our airline again.

▶ If I work as a cabin crew for your airline, while working I will always try to anticipate and respond to the passengers' needs quickly for their safety and comfort. When passengers leaves an aircraft, I will always make sure that they leave with a smile.

외국 항공사 추가질문 – Emotion-Related Questions

1. Have you dealt with picky customer?

🎤 말그대로 까다로운 고객을 다룬적이 있냐는 질문이다. 힘든 고객(difficult customer), 또는 요구 사항이 많은 고객(demanding customer)라고 물어볼 수도 있다.

▶ Yes, I have. When I worked as a waitress, I served a customer who wanted to have a coffee. So I brought her the coffee she ordered. But again, she called me to ask for a cup of water even though her cup was full of water. I thought she might want hot water so I asked her whether she wanted hot water. And she kept asking for something that she already got such as napkins and water. I got confused at first but I thought she might need some more attention from us. So I tried to do my best to meet her needs and I didn't mind being bothered to get her the stuff she wanted over and over again. By the time she left the restaurant she said "I'm not an easy person but I was very satisfied with your kind attitude. Thank you." I was very happy and proud of myself as well.

2. What was the difficult thing to work in the service field?

🎤 이 질문은 국내 항공사에서도 가끔 나오기도 한다. 서비스직에 일하면서 힘들었던 점은 아래 꼬리 질문인 어떻게 해결했는지도 반드시 함께 물어본다는 것이다. 배운 점도 어필하도록 한다.

▶ There are customers who complain about things which are out of my hand. Sometimes people complain about somethings that I can not change, like the bad location of our shop, the price of the food, uncomfortable seats. At first, honestly I couldn't understand why they complain with me those things, so I couldn't respond. That's why I felt stressed to deal with those customers.

- ## How did you solve the problem?

  ▶ Actually, it took time but I realized they have no chance to talk to any-one but me. I am the one who deals with customers so they just say everything even for the things I can not actually do for them. Also, even when they don't expect dramatical change from me but they still just want me and the company to know what they feel uncomfortable about. That's why, I try to show them that I'm listening carefully whatever they say to me. Also, I don't hesitate to say sorry if necessary, even though it's not my fault. I think that's the proper attitude as a staff member.

  ▶ Waiting is something customers hate the most. There is no excuse of making people waiting because that make people upset and unpleas-ant most of times. However, I always have so many customers and all of them hate to wait and still I should be kind to all of them. At first, it wasn't easy to make a balance between being fast and being kind.

- ## How did you solve the problem?

  ▶ Before I worked in the service field, I thought being kind is all about service but I could learn that fast service is also so important for cus-tomers. So, I tried to learn my duty as quick as possible. As a part of that, I brought menu at home and memorized and practiced how to hold many cups and plates. Also, I tried to well manage my time when I deal with customers. I tried not to spend too much time at one table but to look around other tables. However, I don't usually chit chat with customers and tried to finish conversation quickly but I tried to talk with a higher voice than my usual tone and not to forget eye contact with big smile.

- ## 3. How did you deal with picky customer?

  🎙 1번에 대한 꼬리 질문이다. 지원자의 문제해결능력, 서비스 마인드, 배려심 등 다양한 성격을 알아낼 수 있는 질문이라고 하겠다.

▶ Even though I can not offer what they want I think, at least, I should try to find other alternatives. Also, I fully explain what the problem was (why I can not offer what they want at the beginning) and then I give them two choices to choose if they want something different.

4. How did you deal with a rude customer?

🎤 무례한 고객에 대한 질문이다. 많은 지원자들이 어려워하면서도 1번 picky customer와 헷갈려 하는 경우가 있는데 까다롭다고 무례한 고객은 아니다. 이러한 답변을 한다면 자칫 면접자가 예민한 사람으로 비춰질 수 있으니 주의해야 한다. 알면서도 의도적으로 '룰'을 지키지 않는 경우, 폭력적인 행동, 폭언 등을 한 경우가 이에 해당되겠다. 이러한 고객들은 대부분 지원자의 재량으로 해결을 할 수 없는 경우가 많다. 그럼에도 불구하고, 그러한 고객을 최소한 calm down할 수 있게끔 할 수 있는 순발력과 위기 대처능력만 보여주면 된다. 명심할 점은 면접관은 여러분이 '영웅'이 된 답변보다 위기의 상황에서 상사나 동료들에게도 정보를 전달해 도움을 요청할 수 있는 성격의 지원자에게 높은 점수를 준다는 것이다.

▶ I was unhappy that moment of course but I tried to convince myself that the situation could be worse if I showed them how I really felt, If the situation got worse, I might feel really down and stressful afterwards. So, not for them but for myself I tried to control my mind in that moment. I thought that's how I work as a professional. Also, actually there are some customers don't have proper manners but I still can not judge them or even correct them cause that's not what I can do as a staff.

5. Have you received any special service?

🎤 지원자 여러분이 고객으로서 좋은 서비스를 받아 본 적이 있는지에 대한 질문이다. 각자가 생각하고 있는 서비스에 대한 정의와 일관성 있는 답변이면 꼬리질문에도 편할 것이다.

▶ While I traveled abroad, I went to a buffet restaurant. I had water bottle with me and I couldn't bring it in. So I had to leave it with a receptionist before I went into restaurant. When I left, the waitress gave me back the bottle full of water. They noticed that I was a tourist and thought I might need water. I was really impressed and that was the best service I've ever received.

Job of Cabin Crew

 Tip

지원하는 항공사에 대한 기본지식은 숙지하고 있어야 한다. 설립연도, 노선, 마일리지 프로그램, 항공기 보유대수, 코드 쉐어(code share) 그리고 각 항공사의 새 소식을 알아두도록 한다. 면접 전 각 항공사의 홈페이지에 들어가 업데이트된 정보를 숙지하고 새로운 서비스나 수상 내역, 광고 등도 주의 깊게 살펴보도록 한다.

자격요건이나 지원동기 이야기할 때 첫 문장으로 사용하기 유용한 표현

- I believe I have the qualification and skills to be a cabin crew in EK.
- I believe I'm the right person you are looking for.
- I'm confident to say that I'm a good fit for this position.
- You should hire me because I believe that I will be a valuable asset to your company.
- I'm ready to provide to this company the customer service that will keep the passenger satisfied.
- You should hire me because I have the personality and requirements for this position and I feel I will add a certain quality to this job.

마무리에 유용한 표현

- I am very confident about this position.

- I believe that I will be an asset to your company.

- So I'm confident I'll be the best candidate for this position.

- I am ready to provide to this company the customer service that will keep the passenger satisfied.

- I am very passionate about this work and I'll always keep studying to become a great cabin crew if I'm hired by your airline.

- I am reliable and will always be here whenever the company needs my service. I look forward to being a part of your company.

- Most of all, I'm very excited and passionate about this position and will always give my 100%.

- I will always give my best to meet and exceed your expectations.

- I believe my personality, passion and experiences combined make me a wonderful part of team, as well as a valuable asset to the company.

1. Why do you want to work as a cabin crew?

여행이 좋아서, 사람 만나는 것을 좋아해서, 잘 웃어서 등의 흔한 대답보다는 서비스업종에서 일한 경력을 바탕으로 최고의 서비스를 드리고자 지원했다는 식의 구체적이고 비전 있는 답이 요구된다. 외국 항공사의 경우는 '우리 회사'에 지원한 이유를 물어보기 때문에 본인의 지원동기와 자격요건 + 그 회사에 대한 지식 + 포부의 구조로 답변하도록 한다.

▶ I was attracted by the vision of this company and I think I can develop my capabilities and can show my real ability to the full.

▶ My family and friends and whom I know have flown with your airlines. Their experiences have made a good impression on me concerning your airlines. Your company has made a strong impression in comparison to the other carriers. If I'm hired by your company, I'll offer the best service to your passengers.

▶ My career is very important to me. It is what I am most focused on now. I really want this job because I think I can grow up with this company. I want to work hard and be promoted.

▶ When I traveled on your airline, I was impressed with the way the flight attendants worked. I also want to give happiness and pleasant memories to passengers.

▶ I think I can have various experiences as a cabin crew. So, I can keep challenging myself and learning new things through this job. It would be really great for me.

▶ As a cabin crew, I should deal with various passengers and situations on board and in other countries. So, I should think smart and act quickly. To do so, I should utilize my different talents and merits according to different situations, so I believe I can keep challenging myself and I feel this job is attractive for me.

▶ I see one of the most attractive parts of working as a cabin crew is that it offers me a colorful life style. Meeting people from various background, building a friendship with different types of co-workers on the job and experiencing interesting cultures in person would be so exciting to me. I think I will gain plenty of experience and have a fulfilling life.

▶ I would love to give the best service to everyone I meet and give a great impression of Korea. And meeting with all kinds of people from all over the world on the job would be an exciting challenge to me.

▶ I like to work that allows me to come in contact with any people of different backgrounds. I also like to work in the field that provides me make a good use of my service-oriented personality. Most of all, I hope to give a good impression to everyone I meet and offer the best possible service to them while flying in EK I think this job would offer me a lot of emotionally rewarding and fulfilling experiences.

▶ I am very interested in this position because I'm kind of a person who enjoys experiencing and learning about different people and cultures. I am also flexible in relationship to others and in associating with other cultures. I'm proud of myself for this reason. Since a cabin crew's job needs people skills, this aspect of myself may be useful. Most of all, I love to help people and I want to be part of a team. I want to work with many co-workers in a team-oriented environment.

2. Do your parents agree with your wanting to become a flight attendant?

🎙 국내 항공사에서 물어볼 수 있는 질문이다. 간혹 베이스가 외국인 외국 항공사에서는 그 나라에 가서 사는 것에 대해 부모님이 어떻게 생각하시는지에 대해서 물어보기도 한다.

▶ Yes, they support me in this. It's a very competitive job so they have encouraged me to do my best.

3. What is the most important qualification to work as a cabin crew?

What is the most important character for a Flight Attendant?

What is your ideal image of a Flight Attendant?

🎙 본인의 '자격요건'에 대한 간접적인 질문임을 이해해야 한다. 승무원으로서 중요한 요건을 얘기한 후 자신이 그러한 지원자임을 강조하는 것도 좋다.

▶ I think the most important thing is (professionalism / responsibility / flexibility / smart thinking and quick reaction.) Because, as a cabin crew, I should deal with various passengers and situations on board. So, I should (work as a professional / have a strong sense of responsibility / be flexible / think smart and act quickly) on board.

▶ I think cabin crew would need to be intelligent, diligent and multi-skilled. Also they need innovative ideas because sometimes they have to face difficult situation.

▶ In order to serve for many people, it may be necessary to be efficient and energetic.

▶ Being aware of passengers'needs, we need to serve them with a friendly attitude.

▶ Being able to make the right decision and remain calm while on duty.

▶ Flexibility, good health and physical strength seem to be very important.

▶ The job may require warm-heartedness and a positive personality.

🎯 참고 단어　　considerate, kindly, concerned, friendly, generous, obliging, charitable, benign, warm, thoughtful, compassionate, creative, patient, careful, punctual, gentle, sociable

4. What did you prepare to become a cabin crew?

🎙 항공관련학과에 재학 중이거나 졸업한 학생들이라면 학과에서 배운 점과 꾸준한 어학공부, 또한 서비스직에서 아르바이트 경험, 관련 자격증 취득 등 여러 가지 답변을 해도 된다. 다만 인터뷰 연습을 꾸준히 했다는 답변은 자칫 면접관으로 하여금 준비된 답변을 한다는 인상을 주게될 수 있으므로 주의한다.

▶ I attended an English institute to improve my english conversation skill(TOEIC score).

Also, I enjoyed _____ three times a week to keep myself healthy. (sport) Additionally I tried to have a smiling face and right posture all the time.

▶ I attended an English academy to improve my english skill and communication skill. And i did swimming twice a week to keep myself healthy . Also, i visited a lot of countries to understand different culture. Because of these experience, i believe i am well prepared person.

5. What do you know about Korean Air?

🎙 대한항공에 대한 예이지만 국내 항공사 대부분 이런 구조로 답변해도 된다. 최근에 업데이트된 서비스, 수상실적 등은 중요하다. 항상 정보를 업데이트 하도록 한다.

▶ Korean Air has destinations to _____ countries and _____ cities. Recently, it has started flights to _____. Also, it is well known for its world top class cargo, so it won many awards from that part. Even more, it won _____ with its_____.

▶ Therefore, I think Korean Air has already became one the respected leaders in the airline world community.

6. What is the SKY PASS program?(Sky Team, Asiana Club, Star Alliance)

🎙 각 항공사에 마일리지 프로그램은 알고 있는 것이 좋다. 국내 항공사의 경우 지원자의 열정 등을 알 수 있는 질문이기 때문이다.

▶ Mileage rewards per use of services provided by Korean Air and Korean Air affiliates including hotels, rental car services, credit card companies, etc.

▶ Various privileges provided including bonus flight tickets, etc.

▶ Various mileage rewards and bonuses when traveling with Korean Air or any member carrier of the Sky Team Airline Alliance(Aeroflot, Aeromexico, Air France, Alitalia, Continental Airlines, Czech Airlines, Delta Airlines, KLM Royal Dutch Airlines, and Northwest Airlines).

7. Once you become a flight attendant, what kind of service would you like to offer?

🎙 이는 이미 '서비스'에 대해 언급을 하였듯이 자신의 기본적인 서비스 마인드를 보는 질문이다. 일관성 있게 답변하도록 하자.

▶ I want to be a flight attendant to do my best with thinking the passengers safety and comfort every moment without losing calmness and kindness under any situation.

▶ If I become a member of this company which I dreamed to enter, I will become a stewardess who has a warm heart to meet passenger sincerely like as a family.

▶ I will keep smiling and trying to create a friendly atmosphere.

▶ I will try to always keep in mind what kind of service passenger expects to get on board.

▶ I'd like to offer services that satisfy passengers of all ages.

8. What do you know about Asiana Airlines?

▶ Asiana Airlines has destinations to _____ countries and _____cities. Recently, it has started flights to _____. (Recently, it has increased flights to_____.)

Also, it is well known for its high quality in-flight service and cabin crew. It has selected as one of five star airline and won ATW award last year. That's why I believe Asiana is one of the best airlines in the world.

9. What do you know about our company?

🎙 외항사의 경우 누구나 외워서 말할 수 있는 정보보다 새로운 서비스, 또는 회사가 자부심을 가지고 있는 영역에 대해 언급해 주면 좋다. 여기에 덧붙여 최고의 항공사에서 최고의 서비스를 제공하고 싶다는 포부로 끝을 내면 지원자의 열정을 볼 수 있다.

▶ What I've discovered is that your company is firmly established with a long history. Company has continued to grow healthily over the years. OO airlines covers OO cities in OO countries and is one of the best and most well known airlines providing excellent service to its passengers.

▶ OO airlines is growing at an incredible speed. Today you are an international carrier with an expanding network which covers Asia, Europe, North America and Australia. I like to work with various people from all over the world. I heard your company has a good reputation for welfare. If I'm hired by your company, I will be proud to be a member of OO airlines.

10. What is a good point of working as a cabin crew?

🎙 승무원으로 일하게 되면 좋은 점은 많다. 여행 등 외부적으로 얻게 되는 것만 얘기하는 것보다 자신에 대해 조금 더 초점을 맞추어주길 바란다.

▶ As a cabin crew, I can have various experiences on board and in other countries as well. From those experiences, I can keep challenging myself and broaden my perspective. So, I believe I can make better future through this job.

▶ There are so many good point of working as a cabin crew. But one of the greatest advantage of being a cabin crew is that i can see a lot of new place and meet new people. I think it's like a free short holiday. Also, from these experience, i can keep challenging myself.

11. What is a bad point of working as a cabin crew?

🎙 힘든 점은 많이 얘기할 필요가 없다. 자신에게는 전혀 문제가 되지 않는 한 가지 정도를 얘기하자.

▶ As a cabin crew, I should always control my mind and have a smiling face in front of passengers. It might be stressful sometimes to maintain positive face all the time regardless of my personal condition or feeling. However. I fully understand that it is the most basic point of this job, so it might be not easy but I'm able to manage it well.

▶ Cabin crew has very irregular life style according to monthly flight schedule. So, it might be difficult to make long term plans and attend special family events. Sometimes I might feel uncomfortable and disappointed about it. However, there are no perfect job in this world. So, I can manage those feelings with my job satisfaction as a crew.

▶ As a cabin crew, I think I always have smiling face in front of passengers even though I have in bad situation. Sometimes it might be stressful to control my mind. However, I of course understand that it is the most basic point of this job and there are so many good points of working as a cabin crew. So I am able to manage it well.

12. What are some of your career objectives?

🎤 직업관에 대한 질문이다. 직업관에 대해 명확하게 얘기할 수 있는 지원자가 승무원의 직업에 대해서도 이해를 잘할 것이라고 판단이 되는 것은 당연할 것이다.

▶ I want a career that will allow me to continually develop on my existing skills.

▶ When I'm looking for work, I always consider the company's future prospects.

▶ I guess the most important factor is whether or not I find the work interesting. I need to have some level of passion for the work that I'm doing. Otherwise I will eventually lose interest in my work.

13. What are your future plans?

🎤 계획은 단기, 중기, 장기로 나누어 얘기하면 훨씬 주관이 뚜렷해보여 긍정적이다.

▶ My future plan is to be a one of the successful KE/OZ cabin crew. I'll cooperate to create a good working environment that would greatly help the company to progress.

▶ I have a clear goal in mind to achieve success at work as a cabin crew. I will work hard, put in my best effort, be patient, and stay positive.

▶ I think choosing right career is very important. Most of us spend a great part of our lives at our jobs. For that reason we should try to find out what our talents are and how we can use them. Besides I guess working in this field will be suitable for my aptitude.

12

Scenario Questions / Role-Play

 Tip

지원자의 상황 대처 능력과 순발력을 평가하기 위한 롤 플레이 면접은 영어 테스트에서는 가장 어려운 답변이라 할 수 있다. 긴장하지 말고 최선을 다해서 대답하되 외운 티가 나지 않도록 전문적인 단어의 사용이나 실제 승무원과 같은 일처리 식의 답변은 피하는 것이 좋다. 어떠한 상황에서도 승객에 대한 공감, 감정이입이 제일 먼저 나와야 할 것임을 명심하자.

면접관들이 제시한 상황에서 본인이 승무원이라고 가정하고 어떻게 행동할 것인지 연극하듯이 보여줘야 한다. 주로 난처한 질문이 나오므로 당황하지 않는 것이 중요하며, 면접관들을 실제 승객으로 생각하고 침착하고 친절한 모습을 보여주도록 노력한다. 부정적인 답변을 피하고 "찾아보겠습니다. 확인 먼저 해보겠습니다"와 같이 노력하는 모습을 보여주는 것이 좋다. 상황 질문에는 정답이나 오답은 없다. 하지만 지원자들이 얼마나 상식적으로, 또는 합리적으로 예기치 못한 상황을 처리하고 승객들에게 성실하게 그리고 친절하게 도움을 줄 수 있는지를 알아보기 위한 시험적인 질문이다. 어떠한 상황에도, 1. 공감, 감정이입 2. 문제를 해결하려고 하는 성실성, 친절함 3. 꾸준한 관심이 필요하다. 단어나 문장 선택 시 승객의 마음이 상하지 않도록 요령 있게 대처한다. 사용하는 단어의 선택이나 전달하는 태도는 매우 중요하다. 완벽한 답변을 찾기보다는 왜 그렇게 할 것인지 본인의 답변을 논리적으로 풀어간다.

승객의 요구를 거절할 때에나 컴플레인을 처리할 때 유용한 문장과 방법

① 사과(Apology)

1. I'm so sorry. / I'm terribly sorry.

2. I'm very sorry. / I'm afraid that …

3. I'm sorry. I'm afraid that…

4. Please accept our sincere apologies. …

② 감정이입(Showing Empathy)

1. I understand that you have…

2. I understand that you are very unhappy because…

3. I can understand that you are very unhappy because of…

4. I know that you are very upset.

5. I would feel the same way if…

6. I'm sorry that you have had that experience

7. Thank you for bringing the case to our attention

8. We appreciate your feedback for our continuous service improvement.

9. I can understand how you feel.

10. I do understand your situation.

11. I'm sorry you feel that way.

12. I do share your concern

③ 상황 설명(Explaining)

1. But due to … we are not able to…

2. It is a safety reason that passengers are not allowed to…

④ 차선책 제공(Offer An Alternative)

1. May I offer you …? / You may … instead of…

2. I will have to ask you to…

기내 서비스나 상황 대처에 사용하기 유용한 문장들

① 시범을 보일 때(Demonstrating)

Let me show you how to do it. First, … and next … is that alright?

② 음료나 음식을 서비스할 때(Serving Meals)

Here you are, sir/ma'am. Enjoy your meal. What would you like to drink?

③ 난기류 때(During Turbulence)

Remain seated please. The seatbelt sign is on. I'm sorry, sir/ma'am but you'll have to wait.

④ 감압 시(During Decompression)

Pull down the oxygen mask and place over your nose and mouth.

⑤ 난동을 부리는 승객을 다룰 때(Dealing With Disruptive Passengers)

Please stop now, don't shout. You need to sit down and calm down.

1. A passenger wants special meal(vegetarian) but he / she didn't reserve in advance. And catering didn't prepare for extra special meal. What would you say to that passenger?

   🎤 보통은 특별식을 미리 주문하지 않고 채식을 요구하는 승객의 예가 대부분이다. 이럴때에 승무원의 순발력 있는 대처는 기내에서 샐러드, 빵 등을 이용해 채식주의자를 위한 식사를 준비해 드리는 것이다.

   ▶ Sir/Ma'am, I'm afraid there won't be a special meal catered for you. Don't worry, we'll prepare something suitable for you, but it may take a while to prepare your meal.

2. Passenger wants to read English newspaper, but English newspapers have been taken. What would you say?

   🎤 이런 경우 솔직히 말씀드리고 사과를 한 후 다른 대체물(영문 잡지 등)을 먼저 제안해드리는 것도 센스있는 답변이 될 수 있다.

▶ Unfortunately all the English language newspapers have been taken. But I'll get you a copy as soon as one is available.

3. Children running around disturbing other passenger(If a child is noisy and shouts). What would you say to their parents?

🎤 많은 사람들이 이런 경우 주변의 다른 승객들의 입장에서만 생각하고 답변하는 경향이 있다. 그러나 아이 입장, 부모 입장에서도 생각을 해보면 오히려 답이 더 쉬워질 수 있다.

▶ Sir/Ma'am, for the comfort of other passengers, would you please ask your children to return to their seat?

▶ I'll give him some candies or souvenir. If I have time, I'd play with him for a while. If he's still doing, I'd tell the parents that the child's bothering other passengers.

4. What would be your behavior in case of emergency?

🎤 기내에 응급상황에 대해서는 아직은 구체적으로 몰라도 된다. 단지 평정심을 유지하고 침착하게 대응하며 팀 멤버들과의 지속적인 커뮤니케이션을 하는게 중요하다는것은 알고 있어야 한다.

▶ I must try to stay calm and be alert. And then I must try to control any emergency situation so as to protect passengers according to the procedures I've learned in training school and the captain's command.

5. Passenger couldn't get their meal choice, what will you do?

🎤 빈번히 일어나는 일이지만 승무원의 응대에 따라 승객의 기분이 달라진다는것을 명심해야 한다. 사실만을 얘기하는것 보다도 다른 초이스도 아주 맛있으니 꼭 드셔보시라고 권유도 할 수 있는 성격의 승무원이 이런 문제에 대해서 고객의 불평을 덜 받는다.

▶ I will apologize to the passenger first and try to offer another meal using my selling skills. I might explain to the passenger that our other choices are also very delicious and I wouldn't forget to offer some extra care later on.

6. What will you do if your passenger keep insisting to use mobile phone on board?

🎙 안전상의 이유로 이, 착륙시에는 반드시 꺼야한다. 단호하게 얘기할 수 있어야 한다. 하지만 요즘에는 기내 wi-fi 시스템이 있어 비행 중에 스마트폰을 켤 수 있기도 하므로 항공사의 기종, 서비스 등을 미리 알고 답변하는것이 더 센스있어 보인다.

▶ As far as I know, all airlines prohibit the use of mobile phones during take off and landing. I think it is related to safety. So, I'll explain the safety reason and keep requesting not to use it.

▶ Excuse me, sir (ma'am). Would you please turn off your mobile. If you use mobile on board, it might interfere captain's communication with ground and navigation system of aircraft. I totally understand your point, but I still need to prevent little possibility because it is regarding safety issue. I hope you understand. Please let me know if there is anything I can do for you. Thank you for your cooperation.

7. What will you do if your passenger complain about delay?

🎙 항공기 지연의 이유는 여러 가지가 있을 것이다. 기다리는 동안 지루하지 않도록 음료나 신문, 잡지 등의 서비스를 제공하는것 뿐만 아니라 지속적으로 상황 안내방송을 해주는 것이 아주 중요하다.

▶ Waiting is something that all people dislike and it makes people angry. So, I will quickly check the reason for the delay and then inform the passenger. Also, I will offer a drink or a newspaper if he (she) wants while waiting.

▶ I'm sorry but flight has been delayed due to aircraft maintenance. Sorry for your inconvenience. Would you please wait for a while?

▶ Our Engineers doing their best for immediate departure. However, this is all about safety issue, so I hope you understand. As soon as we finish engineering check up, we will take off very shortly. Would you like something to drink while you are waiting? Here you are. Please let me know, if you need anything else. So sorry for all this once again and thank you for your kind understanding.

8. If there is turbulence and the passenger refuse to fasten seat belt, what would you do?

🎤 '안전'과 '고객 서비스' 중에 승객의 안전이 먼저라는 생각이 있다면 승객 스스로의 안전을 위협하는 행동에 대해서는 소신을 갖고 어느 정도 강하게 요청해도 괜찮다.

▶ I would ask him firmly. It's important to keep the passenger safe and make the passenger understand that.

9. If you spill drink to your passenger, how would you handle that situation?

🎤 뜨거운 음료, 와인 등 여러가지 상황이 있을 수 있다. 와인을 쏟았을 때 기내에 있는 아이템으로 얼룩을 지울 수 있는 예는 탄산수(Soda water)를 이용하면 된다. 드라이클리닝 쿠폰 제공 등은 여러분의 재량으로 해결할 수 있는 솔루션이 아니므로 답변에 유의한다.

▶ If it is a hot drink, I'll check whether the passenger is burned or not. Then, I'll get some dry towels. Also, I would apologize sincerely because it is totally my mistake. Lastly, I would keep monitoring the passenger whether everything is in good condition.

10. What would you do with a passenger who is out of control?

🎤 중요한 포인트는 이 상황에서는 여러분이 수퍼맨이 되어 해결하는 답변이 아니라 그 고객을 어떻게 평정심을 유지하도록 하는것과 도움이 필요할 때에 동료에게 적극적으로 도움을 요청할 수 있는 마인드이다.

▶ First of all, I'll try to have maximum patience. Then, I'll ask what the matter is in a very polite way and try to deal with the situation instantly. If a passenger is out of control though, I'll require help from my senior who has much more experience than me.

11. How can you help mothers with children on the flight?

🎙 아이의 입장에서 그리고 엄마의 입장에서 생각하고 답변하도록 하자. 아이 케어를 위한 편의를 제공해주고 기내에 장난감 등도 제공해주며 기내 게임 등 즐길 수 있는 것들을 아이에게 세세히 설명해주는것도 좋다.

▶ I can imagine that it's not easy to travel with children, I think I will help her like any other passenger. But of course, I think I will give more attention to her children and assist a mother when she needs my help. I will try my best to make sure both the mother and her children have a comfortable flight.

12. If drunken passenger keep requesting for more drinks, how would you handle this situation?

🎙 이 질문은 이미 술 취한 고객일 경우이다. 하지만 고객 입장에서 술을 이미 많이 마셨다라고 하면 기분이 나쁠 수 있으므로 여러분의 서비스 마인드와 people skill을 이용하여 차선책을 제공하는 것 등도 좋은 답변이 될 것이다.

▶ Even though the passenger is already drunk, I can not say he looks drunk or refuse his request. So, I'll just try to slow down his speed and offer some non alcoholic drinks. "Sir, I know you feel completely OK now, but how about having some rest for now (having some other cold beverage for now) and take another drink after a while? I don't think you are drunk now but people usually get drunk 10 times easier during the flight."

13. If one of your passengers is sick, what should you do?

🎙 어떠한 해결책을 제시하는 것보다 제일 먼저 승무원이 침착해야 한다는 점이 중요하다. 그리고 승객의 상황을 살피고 다른 승무원과 정보 공유를 반드시 해야한다. 그런 뒤에 상황이 나아지지 않는다면 기내에 의사나 간호사를 찾는 안내방송을 한다.

▶ I think I should give full attention to the passenger. And I have to know what his/her condition is. If it is just a slight fever or cold, I'll go and ask if anything is needed. If the passenger is sick with a chronic condition, my colleague and I would have to give more attention to the passenger. I will do my best by giving the right treatment for a sick passenger with my colleague. If there is a doctor or nurse who can help a sick passenger, we might ask for help. I think I should study hard about first aid in a training class.

14. What would you do if a passenger smoke in the airplane?

🎤 승객의 안전이 위협되는 상황이고 항공법에 위배되는 행동이므로 단호하게 얘기하여 반복되지 않도록 해야 한다. 그런 다음 비행이 끝날 때까지 계속해서 예의주시하겠다는 답변도 좋다.

▶ First of all, I'd tell the passenger not to smoke in the aircraft because it is dangerous. Then I would offer some sweet candy or chocolate to the passenger to forget about smoking. I'd also remember to inform the other crew members because as a team, I think it is important information to share. If he continues to smoke, I'd be assertive this time and explain again on behalf of the crew, not to smoke in the airplane as it may cause a fire on board and it is against the law. Service is important but I think the passenger's safety is a priority. Then I'd inform the crew members again and keep monitoring the passenger.

15. If your passenger wants your phone number, how would you handle this situation?

🎤 상대방을 기분 나쁘지 않게 거절하는 방법, 이 또한 지원자의 people skill을 알아보는 질문이다.

▶ I think he is asking me for my phone number because he got a good impression from me. So, I'd say thank you, but politely refuse his request. However, if he keeps asking for my number then I'd receive his business card instead.

16. What would you do if a passenger refuses to stow his baggage in the overhead bin?

🎤 승객의 안전과 관련된 질문은 단호하게 얘기하되 그 이유를 상세히 고객에게 설명해주면 된다.

▶ I understand that he might have a reason why he doesn't want to. But, because of passenger safety I would tell him that it is not safe to hold his bag. If there is turbulence the bag might hurt him. For that safety reason I would ask him once again to put his bag inside the overhead bin.

17. How would you handle an angry passenger?

🎤 아무 이유없이 화를 내는 고객은 없을 것이다. 고객 입장에서 생각해보고 고객의 말을 끝까지 잘 들어주는 것만으로도 고객은 평정심을 찾을 수 있다. 어떠한 해결책을 제시하는 것보다 고객입장에서 잘 들어주고 감정이입을 해주는 것이 훨씬 효과적이다.

▶ I would apologize for his/her inconvenience. And I think I would let the passenger talk and just listen carefully so that I can understand what his/her problem is. Then I'd try to find a solution. If I found one I would be very happy to help my passenger. However, if there is no right solution for that problem, I would explain the situation and offer alternatives because I want to make my passenger feel better.

18. What would you do if a passenger asks for an extra meal?

🎤 추가로 식사를 요청하는 고객에게는 여러 가지 솔루션이 있을 수 있겠다. 중요한 점은 모든 고객에게 식사 제공이 끝난 후에 가능하다는 점이다. 하지만 그 전에 계속 요구하는 고객에게는 추가로 빵이나 기내에 탑재된 스낵 정도를 제공해 드린 뒤 식사 서비스가 끝날 때까지 기다려달라고 얘기한다.

▶ I think I would tell him that I can let him know until after finishing the meal service whether we have an extra meal or not. And I would ask my senior if I can serve one to my passenger. If she says yes, I would serve it pleasantly, or If I can't, I would go to my passenger and say sorry we don't have any extra meals left over. However I would find alternatives such as bread rolls or other snacks available on board.

13

Self-PR

Tip

자기소개의 경우 최대한 수식어와 불필요한 말을 줄여 의미 전달이 잘 이루어지도록 해야 한다. 따라서 한글 자기소개를 그대로 영문으로 번역하려는 것은 금물이다. 자신의 경험을 모두 되새겨 본 후 그 중 가장 이야기 하고 싶은 것 한 가지 혹은 두 가지만 선정하여 이에 대해서 서술하도록 한다. 본인에 대해서 가장 강조하고 싶은 것을 앞에서 준비한 성격, 아르바이트 경험, 해외 경험, 여행 경험, 학교 전공, 동아리 활동, 자원 봉사, 자격증, 수상 경력 등 중에서 선택해 보자.

- My name is 000. I'm a responsible and approachable person. During my university days, I worked at a family restaurant for 6 months. That time, I wore uniform and my name badge all the time, so I always tried to fully in charge of my part and offer best service to my customers. Also, I've been to Europe for traveling. At first, I was bit shy to say hello first and talk to people who I first met. However, I became more approachable person through my experiences there. I believe I can be one of the asset of your company with these personalities. Thank you.

- I graduated from Korea University. My major was engineering. I'm working for the _____ hotel. I'm 25 years old and live in Yeuksam-Dong with my family.

My hobbies are swimming and playing bowling. I can say I'm an active and positive person. I have many friends and get along well with them. When I decide to do something, I always try to do my best.

- I was born in Busan, but grew up in Seoul for most of my life. I come from an average middle class family and had a happy childhood. But unlike most of my friends, I had to pay my college tuition because my father wanted me to earn my own through school for independence. I had many part-time jobs throughout my university days and I learned a lot about life and the importance of job.

- I think I'm a pretty easy person to get along with. I love meeting new people, and I also like exciting outdoor activities such as soccer and basketball. So, one of my biggest strengths is that I have the ability to deal with every type of person. Particularly, I am very interested in travelling and I've been to more than half of the cities in my country. I have also been to Greece, France, and several other countries in Europe. I love to experience various cultures, meet people, and see fantastic places. No matter where I go, there are people who can teach me things that I will never forget. That's why I enjoy traveling. It has also provided me with a good basic knowledge of the tourism industry.

- I'm a person who has sharing mind and customer-oriented attitude. I majored in hotel management, so I could learn service mind and customer handling skills. Also, I've been participated in volunteer works with my family members for two years. We visit welfare center regularly and give a hand and spend time with the elderly staying there. From these experiences, I can say that I am a person who your company is looking for. Thank you.

- I love to experience and learn new things. So, I worked in various places including restaurants, department store and amusement park. Through different experiences, I could learn how to deal with various customers and make a good team work with many co-workers. I can confidently say that I can really enjoy my job and develop myself as a member of your company with my challenging mind and passion. Thank you.

- I am the type of person who always tries to see the positive side of things. One of my favorite saying is, "Do your best, and God will do the rest." If I try my best, I believe the result will be positive. Besides, I have good interpersonal skills. I'm easy to get along with and have a good sense of humor. I believe those my personalities are suitable for this job.

- I believe that I am a very sociable and reliable person. I can make friends easily and enjoy mixing with them. That's why I have many good friends around me and keep a good relationship with them. And I've been to Australia to study English for 6 months. It was really good chance for me not only to improve my English skill, but to make lots of local friends and learn their cultures. Also, I have many part-time job experiences in service field. Through these experiences, I gained service mind and became more independent.

- I was born in Seoul and raised in Busan. I graduated from Korea University with a Master's degree in Philosophy last year. I'm working for the _____ company. I enjoy playing computer games and watching sports.

- Thank you for giving me a chance to introduce myself. My name is _____. I was born in 1996 and grew up in Seoul. I graduated Korea University in February this year. I like classical music and also like to play tennis.

- My name is Park Sun-Young. I am a twenty-year-old sophomore college student. I live in Seocho-dong, Seoul. I like to read and go to the movies. I also like sports, especially bowling. I can speak English and Japanese fluently. I am fairly outgoing person. I hope to get a job where can travel and meet a lot of people.

Resume / Cover Letter

 영문 이력서 구성 요소

Resume에 정해진 양식이 있는 것은 아니지만 보는 사람으로 하여금 지원자에 대하여 금방 파악할 수 있도록 간단하고 명료하게 작성한다. 자신이 얼마나 우수한 인재이며, 얼마만큼 회사에 공헌할 수 있겠는가에 대해 강한 인상을 심어주어야 한다.

① **Personal Data**(Identifying Information)

이름, 주소, 전화번호, 생년월일, 성별 등을 기록한다. 첫줄 상단에 이름을 적고 그 아래에 현주소와 연락처, 전화번호, 기타 인적사항을 적는다. 나이(Date of Birth)는 '월, 일, 년' 순으로 적으면 되고 본적과 현주소를 기재할 때는 '번지, 통, 반, 구(면), 시(도)' 순으로 적고 끝에 우편번호도 적는다.

② **Job Objective**(Career Objective)

희망하는 직종과 직무를 기재하며 Goal이라고도 한다. 이 부분은 지원자의 직업목표를 밝히는 항목으로 희망직종, 분야 혹은 부서를 나열하는 방법을 사용하기도 한다. 이때는 해당 기업의 Organizational Chart(부서기구)를 알아보고 희망하는 해당부서가 있는지의 여부를 확인한다. 지원자가 찾는 부서 또는 해당 포지션의 이름을 확인할 수 없을 경우는 자신의 적성과 전공 지식을 활용할 수 있는 분야에서의 근무를 원한다고 적으면 된다.

③ Summary of Qualifications(Capabilities)

희망직무에 대응하는 능력과 자질을 기재한다.

④ Professional Work Experience(Employment)

원칙적으로 최근의 것으로부터 과거로 거슬러 올라가면서 적는다. 특히 경력자인 경우는 우리말 이력서와는 반대로 경력을 학력보다 먼저 적는다. 학생일 경우는 아르바이트 경험을 적는다. 학벌이나 자격증보다는 경력, 능력을 중시하며 채용하는 외국인 회사에 지원할 경우 가장 중요한 부분이다. 기업에서 필요로 하는 업무내용과 관계없는 경력을 되도록이면 간소화시키고 관련 있는 경력 등을 위주로 기술하는 것이 좋다.

⑤ Education(Educational History)

특별한 요구가 없는 한 최종학력만을 적으면 된다. 전문대나 대학졸업자이면 초등학교, 중학교 등은 적을 필요가 없다. 대학원 졸업인 경우에는 대학 학력부터 적는다. 미국식 기재방식은 최종 졸업학교부터 적는 것이 원칙이나 한국식으로 과거부터 최근 순으로 적어도 무방하다. 졸업년도와 학교, 학위명을 적고 부전공과 졸업 학점이 본인에게 유리하다면 덧붙이고, 부전공 사항은 졸업 또는 졸업 예정란 뒤에 괄호를 사용하여 'Minor is Business Administration'이라고 쓰면 된다.

⑥ Honors and Awards(Additional Remarks)

상벌관계도 역시 교내외적인 행사에서의 수상경력이나 각종 표창경력을 기록한다. 특기사항란으로 국문이력서와 마찬가지로 국가적으로 공인된 자격증이나 면허증 발급사항을 기재한다. 참고로 영어교사 자격증을 취득(또는 취득 예정)한 사람의 경우라면 'Will be Awarded Teaching Certification of English teacher given by the Ministry of Education in 2025'이라고 작성하면 된다. 한 가지 유의할 점은 resume에서는 'What I did' 식의 과거형 보다는 'What I can do for you'라는 표현을 쓰는 것이 좋은 인상을 남긴다.

⑦ Activities and Volunteer Works

학교에서의 동아리활동과 자원봉사 등 사회활동을 요약해서 쓴다. 요즘에는 자원봉사활동을 적극적으로 평가하는 기업이 많아지고 있다.

⑧ References

이력서에는 우선 Available on request 또는 Furnished promptly upon request(요구 시 즉시 제출하겠음)라고 적어두면 된다. 일반적으로 경력자라면 이전 근무처의 상사나 대학 지도교수 등의 연락처를 쓰면 되고 별도의 양식은 없다. 졸업예정자의 경우 지도 교수나 선배, 프로젝트 수행 경험 시 책임자급으로 하면 무난하다. 신원보증인이라기 보다는 본인의 능력이나 자질에 대해 보증할 수 있는 제3자를 말하며, 부모 형제나 친척은 해당되지 않는다.

물론 위에 언급한 항목들 모두 빠짐없이 적어야 하는 것은 아니다. 자신에게 맞게 적절히 취사선택해도 되고, 또 순서가 자기가 가장 강조하고 싶은 요소를 앞으로 가져가는 등 앞뒤를 바꿔도 무방하다. 단 개인정보(이름, 주소, 전화번호, 희망직종, 학력, 경력 등)와 같은 6가지 요소는 빠짐없이 기재해야 한다. 첫 장 우측 상단에 사진 붙이는 것 또한 필수요소이다.

영문 이력서 작성 시 유의 사항

외국 항공사는 이력서를 단순히 형식적으로 받는 것이 아니라 지원자가 모집분야에 적합한지 여부를 일차적으로 판단하는 수단으로 활용한다. 즉 이력서를 통해 지원자의 능력을 체크하기 때문에 면접시간을 줄인다는 효율적인 생각 방식을 가지고 있는 것이다. 따라서 항공사가 원하는 것은 어떠한 자격요건을 갖추고 있으며, 맡게될 일을 얼마나 잘 수행할 것인지 등이므로 직무내용과 직접적으로 관련 있는 내용에 초점을 맞춰 솔직하게 작성하는 기술이 필요하다.

① 커버레터로 자신을 PR하라

인사 담당자들은 커버레터를 읽은 후 지원자의 이력서를 읽을지 여부를 판단하는 수단으로 활용하고 있기 때문에 영문 이력서 작성 시 반드시 커버레터를 첨부해야한다. 특히, 인사담당자가 외국인이라면 경력을 시간 순으로 나열한 한국식 이력서대신 커버레터가 붙은 이력서를 제출하는 것이 좋으며, 인사담당자의 관심을 끌 수있도록 자신을 최대한 홍보해야 한다.

② 지원동기 및 분야를 분명히 밝혀라

단순히 외국 항공사에 입사하고 싶다는 생각에 어느 분야에 지원해야 하는지 결정도 하지 못한 채 이력서를 제출해서는 안되며, 지원동기에 대한 뚜렷한 명분을 설명, 인사담당자가 수긍할 수 있도록 해야 한다. 지원동기에는 인맥을 활용하거나 기업 홈페이지를 통해 기업의 성향, 기업정신, 인재상 등을 파악해 지원회사에 대한 관심도를 표명하는 것이 좋으며, 구체적이고 간단명료하게 작성해야 한다. 또한 외국계 기업에서는 정확한 지원 분야를 명시하지 않은 경우 자신만의 전문 분야가 없다고 판단하기 때문에 자신이 희망하는 분야를 반드시 밝혀주어야 한다. 정확한 지원분야를 명시하지 않을 경우 이 분야, 저 분야에도 해당되기 때문에 입사 기회의 폭이넓어진다고 생각하는 것은 착각이다.

③ 지원하는 회사와 업무에 맞춰 작성하라

외국계 회사는 즉각적으로 현장에 투입될 수 있는 인재를 중요시하기 때문에 학벌보다는 실무능력과 순발력을 중시한다. 따라서 모집분야에 적합한 경험과 자격을 갖춘 사람을 우선적으로 채용한다. 즉, 직원 모집 시 업무의 범위나 직책이 처음부터 명확하게 정해져 있기 때문에 해당 업무에 맞는 실력을 이미 갖추고 있는 사람만을 선발한다. 따라서 무슨 일이든 다 잘할 수 있다는 식의 의욕보다는 업무에 맞는 실력을 이미 갖추고 있다는 점을 분명하게 입증하는 것이 중요하며, 자신의 경험과 자격이 지원하는 기업에서 모집하고 있는 직종이나 직책에 딱 맞는 적임자라는 것에 초점을 맞춰 이력서를 작성해야 자신을 효과적으로 홍보할 수 있다.

④ 현실성 있는 비전을 제시하라

자신의 비전, 포부가 없는 사람은 발전 가능성이 없어 보이며 자신감이 결여되어 보인다. 능력 위주로 철저히 사람을 뽑는 외국계 기업의 경우 자신의 미래에 대한 비전을 제시하지 못하는 지원자는 당연히 탈락하게 된다. 설사 영어 실력이 다소 부족하더라도 자기 분야에서 전문적인 능력을 갖추고 있으며 자신만의 꿈이 있다고 자신감을 피력한다면 인사담당자의 관심을 끄는데 성공할 수 있을 것이다.

⑤ 경력자의 경우 구체적인 수치를 통해 실적을 설명하라

입사지원 시 자신의 능력을 객관적으로 뒷받침할 수 있는 자료나 근거를 보여주는 것이 필요하다. 따라서 자신의 능력을 구체적인 사례를 통해 밝히는 것이 가장 효과적이다. 전 직장에서 발휘한 성과에 대해 구체적인 사례를 들어 설명한다면 인사담당자의 신뢰를 받을 수 있다.

⑥ 자신만의 색깔을 찾아라

평범하고 모범적인 사람보다는 창의적이고 긍정적이며 적극적인 인재를 선호하기 때문에 단순히 학벌이 높은 것보다는 남다른 이력을 갖고 있는 것이 취업에 성공할 확률이 높다. 따라서 자신만의 독특한 색채를 이력서에 반영해야 한다. 남들과 다른 아르바이트 경험을 갖고 있다든지 자신만의 독특한 생활 철학이 있다면 그러한 사실에 대해 이력서에 기술하는 것이 좋다.

⑦ 공백기간 동안의 실적을 밝혀라

실직은 무능력하다는 것을 말하는 것이 아니다. 따라서 경력상 자신의 공백기간이 있다고 해서 그 기간을 숨기려 하거나 아예 기재하지 않으면 안된다. 솔직하게 공백기간이 있었음을 밝히고 그 공백기간 동안 자신의 발전을 위해서 어떠한 노력을 했으며 어떠한 경험을 쌓았는지 알려야 한다. 그리고 그 공백기간이 자신에게 어떠한 영향을 주었는지 그리고 그러한 경험과 영향이 지원 분야에 어떻게 기여할 수 있는지 등에 대해서도 설명해야 한다.

⑧ 능력과 경력에 초점을 맞춰라

외국계 기입은 국내 기업처럼 출신 학교 등의 학벌이 전혀 중요하지 않으며, 인재 채용 시 지원자의 경험, 경력, 업무수행 능력을 평가해 기업에 기여할 수 있는 인재인지를 판단한다. 따라서 지원하는 분야와 관련 있는 경력 또는 경험이 구체적으로 해당 업무와 어떠한 연관성이 있으며 해당 업무에 투입되었을 경우 어떻게 업무를 수행해 기업에 기여할 수 있는지 등을 밝혀주어야 한다. 그러나 해당 직무와 관련 없는 경력들을 나열하는 것은 좋지 않다. 아르바이트 경험이라도 지원하고자 하는 분야와 관련 있는 사항은 기재하는 것이 좋으며 해당직무와 관련 있는 자격증, 교육수강, 동아리 활동 등도 플러스 요인이 될 수 있다.

⑨ 사소한 것까지 신경 써라

외국계 회사는 자신을 철저하게 관리할 수 있는 능력을 갖춘 사람을 선호하므로 자신이 차분하고 꼼꼼해서 주어진 업무는 실수 없이 완벽하게 소화할 수 있다는 인상을 주어야 한다. 따라서 이력서 작성 시 세심한 주의를 기울여야 한다. 아무리 사소한 것이라도 그냥 지나쳐서는 안되며 틀린 철자나 문법적으로 오류가 있는 문장은 없는지 등도 확인해야 한다. 한 장 이상의 이력서인 첫 장의 맨 끝에 More, Continued를, 두 번째 장 상단에 Page two를 적는 등 세심한 주의를 기울이는 것도 플러스 점수를 받을 수 있다.

⑩ 한국의 실정을 반영하라

인사담당자가 모두 외국인인 것은 아니며, 한국인인 경우도 많다. 이 경우 외국 기업에 근무하기 때문에 좀 더 객관적으로 사람을 뽑기는 하지만 기본 마인드는 한국인의 사고방식을 갖고 있다. 따라서 국문 이력서와는 달리 영문 이력서에는 자신의 신상, 학력사항 등에 대해 작성할 필요가 있다. 단순히 자신의 학력과 신상, 가족사항을 장황하게 늘어놓을 필요는 없지만 핵심적인 것, 인사담당자가 알 필요가 있는 사항은 기재해야 한다. 가령 기혼인지 미혼인지, 여성인지 남성인지 등에 대한 사항은 인사담당자가 기본적으로 파악하고 있어야 하는 내용이다. 최근에는 국내 기업 중에도 직무에 따라 영문 이력서를 요구하는 경우가 많으므로 한국의 실정을 반영하여 이력서를 작성하는 연습이 필요하다.

영문 이력서 구성 요소 별 Sample Sentences

◉ PERSONAL DATA

HYE JIN LEE

104 Dong 303 Ho, Min APT, Seoch Dong,

Seoul, Korea.

(Mobile) + 82 10 1649 9999

E-mail : beautifulife@naver.com

◉ OBJECTIVE

> Example 1

Objective is to secure a cabin crew's position where I get an opportunity to learn and get knowledge about aviation and service field.

> Example 2

Looking for the greatest opportunity to work as a cabin crew for a reputed company.

> Example 3

To utilize my skills and experience as a cabin crew in your one of the finest airlines in the world.

> Example 4

Willing to work as cabin crew with a large national airline.

Example 5

A talented, qualified and self-motivated Flight Attendant.

Example 6

To obtain a position as a professional flight attendant in a well known airlines services.

Example 7

To seek the position of a cabin crew at a well-liked airline company and advance my airline career.

Example 8

Looking an opportunity that will lead to my personal development and give me a chance to prove myself in adding value to the prosperity of the company.

◉ SUMMARY OF QUALIFICATIONS

- Good knowledge about loan items, funding and financial budgets.

- Excellent communication and writing skills.

- Good organizational skills.

- Having strong analytical and organizational skills.

- Excellent ability to understand and follow a set of procedures.

- Excellent communication, written and interpersonal skills.

- Able to work with older people, families and disabled people.

- Having relevant subject knowledge skills.

- Responsible for other duties as assigned.

- Proficient with computer literate such as Microsoft Word, Microsoft Excel, Power point and Internet.

- Excellent experience as a service provider in service industry.

- Excellent ability to work with all levels of internal management and staff, vendors and customers.

- Excellent English communication and writing skills.

- Having strong interpersonal and customer service skills. Extremely pleasant personality with the advent of good physique.

- Excellent communication skills with absolute politeness in verbal communication.

- Immense exposure to the fast paced and high profile work environment through past work experiences.

- Vast air experience preceded by two years of formal training

- Good customer service skills with orientation of complete customer satisfaction.

- Proper communication and coordination with other team members.

- Complete and neat information of the safety measures to be applied in case of emergency situations.

◉ PROFESSIONAL WORK EXPERIENCES

Example 1

Vons Co. Carlsbad, California (02/07/2010 - 04/08/2015)
Office Assistant

- Done duties such as taking phone calls, taking messages, respond to inquiries and provide clerical and secretarial support to center staff and management.

- Responsible for processing maintenance requests for manager and supporting staff.

- Help in bookkeeping, payroll and A/R and A/P processing.

- Responsible for handling daily staff scheduling.

- Help in opening and closing of facility at the beginning and ending of each day.

- Responsible for organizing, registering and publicizing staff for workshops and staff development.

- Reviewed letter and reports and put together in standardized templates.

- Proficient with computer literate such as Microsoft Word, Microsoft Excel, Power point and Internet.

- Ability to use scanner.

- Having knowledge of presentation binding equipment and copiers.

- Able to train new staff.

- Done other duties as needed. (Responsible for other duties as needed.)

Example 2

Landstar Ltd. Forth Worth, Texas
Executive Assistant

- Responsible for managing all executive level administrative tasks that includes conference calls, meetings and arrangement of travel.

- Provide information to incoming calls and respond to internal requests on timely manner.

- Helped in development of reports and presentations of executive levels.

- Responsible for developing innovative records management system for progressing executive travel related accounting documentation.

- Confidential and sensitive information is handled very carefully.

- Responsible for meeting persons, special interest groups and others for management.

- Done other duties as assigned.

San Mateo Public Library
Executive Assistant

- Responsible for leaving demand orders for books and other teaching materials.

- Managed and organized meetings or conferences for the library.

- Helped the Head Librarian to schedule their lecture.

- Manage the scheduling of book signers and guest speakers.

- Responsible for recording documents and presentations in Microsoft Office programs.

Example 3

Watts Pharmaceuticals, Atlanta, GA
Administrative Assistant

- Responsible for handling all official company correspondence.

- All company documents are typed.

- Responsible for typing all company correspondences.

- Give training for new employee.

- Responsible for upgrading office filing system.

- Responsible for other duties as assigned.

Martitta Chamber of Commerce, Martitta, GA
Administration Assistant

- Responsible for typing all company documents and correspondences.

- Responsible for organizing the Annual Marietta chamber Gala.

- Responsible for production of company's bi-monthly newsletter.

- Responsible for answering phones and other enquiries.

- Ability to perform administrative and office support activities.

- Excellent communication and writing skills.

- Able to keep project on schedule.

- Able to update and delegated detail and all projects.

- Able to handle incoming calls and requests.

- Ability to do research, draft and abstract reports.

Example 4

ABC Company, Kauai, Hawaii, (2009–Present)
Administrative Assistant

- Ensured that the shipment orders were with the right carriers and out on the floor.
- Worked with other team players for providing exact shipping details.
- Prepared weekly spreadsheets, travel documents.
- Answered phone and sent e-mails to several supervisors across the country
- Dealt with travel arrangements, mining plans, filing, accumulate ideas for better system for out going and in coming files.

XYZ Ltd, Honolulu, Hawaii (2014–2015)
Administrative Assistant

- Handled various projects with Educational Field services and the Mine Safety and Health Administrations(MSHA). Also responsible for Fed Ex shipments.
- Able to effectively work under pressure and with time limits.
- Extra tasks include updating client's records and updating inventory database.
- Ordered office supplies, performed research as needed, produced and handled customer invoicing and performed receptionist functions.

Example 5

W Hotel, Seoul, Korea. (2009 - 2015)
Assistant Front Office Manager

- Responsible for supervising 40 employees at a 1500 room property. Trained Dual-Rate supervisor, Grave supervisor and agents.

- Processed all the paperwork for the newly hired employees including guest satisfaction performance test, job description, scheduling orientation, orientation checklist, and 90 day probationary period evaluation.

- Responsible for customer service technique and department scheduling. In May 2007 elected as Dept CSA Ambassador and property LMS Super User.

- Completed all Unemployment, State Disability and salary verification inquiries. Kept weekly updates of job openings and placements. Made reservations for the short lived guests for the satisfaction of the guests and ensuring the hotel's budget.

XYZ Hotel & Casino, Frisco, Colorado (2011-2015)
Operations Supervisor

- Responsible for reservations for the short lived guests for the satisfaction of the guests and ensuring the hotel's budget.

- Created employee incentive program and responsible for office supply-ordering. Supervised daily functions of department facilitating 3,100 uniformed employees.

Example 6

Jagson Airlines, Columbia Falls, MT (03/03/2010 - Present)
Cabin Crew

- Assuring comfort and safety to passenger every time.

- Performing security sweeps and safety checks on board.

- Before the plane takes-off demonstrated safety features of aircraft.

- Helped cabin crew with the in-flight meals and beverages service.

- Providing bureau de change facility and in-flight shopping service.

- Trained in first aid techniques.

- Assisted parents with small children to assure enough comfort at all time.

Jet Airways, Wolf Point, MT (03/03/2014 - 09/09/2014)
Cabin Crew

- Helped cabin crew in the verification of safety measures and implementation of safety procedures.

- Provided excellent service to each and every passenger.

- Demonstrated safety instructions before take off and landing.

- Provided an in-flight meal and beverage service and duty to all passengers.

- Ensured passenger satisfaction by resolving problems or disputes.

- Provided assistance to the ground staff on check-in desks and reservations.

- Trained in first aid techniques. Providing excellent customer service so that all the guests can safely enjoy flying.

- Worked with other flight attendants while boarding into the plane to handle passengers of multi nationalities and multicultural background.

Example 7

XYZ Airlines, Richmond, VA(02/02/2014-Present)
Cabin Crew

- Attending the preflight meetings and noting down all the instructions about special passengers such as people suffering from respiratory diseases, celebrities, etc.

- Monitoring the cleanliness and the safety points in the plane before allowing entry to the passengers.

- Welcoming the passengers on the board and greeting them with small conversations.

- Helping the passengers to find their seats

- Reporting the supervisors about any serious issues regarding the seating issues

- Serving the passengers food/drinks promptly and as per their demands

- Checking the seat belts of each passengers just before the plane takes off

- Greeting each passenger at the end of the journey

- Maintaining the plane reports and submitting it to the supervisors

EDUCATION

- Mount Allison University, Hamilton, MT2010 - 2014BA in Languages & Communications.

- South Mountain High School, Helena, MT2006 - 2010High School Diploma.

- Completed post graduate diploma in cabin crew from the Fly Airhostess Institute, Richmond, VA(2014).

LANGUAGES AND OTHER SKILLS

- Computer skills : Proficient with MS Office, Microsoft Excel, Power Point and Internet

Languages

- Spanish Conversational - Limited

- English Fluent - Wide Knowledge

외국 항공사 Cover Letter 쓰기

Cover Letter는 Resume와 함께 보내는 자기소개서로서, 일종의 자기 PR문이라고 할 수 있다. Cover Letter는 Resume의 내용을 보충하고 채용담당자에게 효과적으로 접근하기 위한 편지이다. Resume가 지원자 본인의 전체상을 항목별로 쓴 형식으로 알리는 객관적인 자료라고 하면 Cover Letter는 자신이 그 회사에 얼마나 필요한 인재인가를 문장으로 표현하는 것이다. Cover Letter는 우리나라에는 없는 관습이므로 낯설게 느껴질 수 있으나 압축된 내용을 통해 자신을 효과적으로 홍보하고 회사의 인사담당자로부터 관심을 얻어 Resume 단계로 넘어가기 위한 일종의 요약 소개서/지원 취지서라고 보면 된다. 외국계 회사에서는 채용담당자가 지원 서류를 받을 때 가정 먼저 읽는 것이 Cover Letter이며 Cover Letter의 내용이 부실하거나 Cover Letter가 아예 없을 경우 Resume를 읽어보지도 않는다는 사실을 잊지 말자. 외국 항공사 Cover Letter는 항공사에서 양식을 정해 배포하지 않기 때문에 일정한 양식은 없다. Cover Letter는 국문이력서를 영어로 그대로 번역해서 제출하는 것이 아니기 때문에 어떤 내용으로 써야 하는지 잘 모르는 지원자들이 많다. Cover Letter는 장황하게 쓰는 것은 금물이며 내용을 A4용지의 2/3 정도의 분량으로 작성한다. 우선 Cover Letter에 작성 시 주의하여야 할 내용들은 아래와 같다.

- 동양 문화권에서의 겸양의 미덕은 통하지 않음

- 자기가 가지고 있는 자격, 능력, 경험이 지원 직종에 어떻게 적합한지 강조

- 그 회사와 직종에 대하여 강한 관심을 가지고 있는지 표현

- 상대방의 관심을 끌어 지원자를 만나보고 싶다고 여기게 할 정도의 영어 표현력 요구

- Cover Letter를 통하여 영어실력 자체도 평가됨

- 한 페이지 이내로 간결하게 작성

- 속어나 문법에 어긋나는 표현 및 오타 절대 금지

- 초점이 흐린 장황한 긴 문장은 오히려 역효과

- Cover Letter라는 제목을 쓰지 말 것(Cover Letter인지 모두가 알고 있음)

- 구성요소는 주소와 날짜, 수취인명, 인사, 본문, 맺는 말, 성명 및 서명의 순서

1. 우측 상단에는 나의 정보(주소, 연락처 등)를 기입한다.

2. 좌측 하단에는 인사담당자의 정보에 대해 입력한다. 인사담당자의 이름과 주소, 연락처를 기입하고, 혹시 인사담당자의 정보를 모르는 경우에는 Dear Recruiting Manager, 또는 Dear Hiring Manager로 쓰면 된다.

3. 이제 본격적인 내용을 기입할 '서론' 부분이다. 지원하고자 하는 동기와 본론에서 전개할 내용들을 적으면 된다. 본론에서 소개할 자신의 장점 키 포인트를 포함한 간단한 자기소개를 하고 그 항공사의 어떤 점에 끌렸는지, 어떻게 도움이 되고 싶은지 등을 작성하면 된다.

4. 서론에 이은 '본론'은 가장 중요한 부분이다. 본론에서는 자신의 장점을 나타낼 수 있는 단어와 그 장점을 뒷받침 할 수 있는 간단한 사례(구체적인 경험이나 실제 수치, 수상 경력 등)으로 이루어진다. 즉 면접에서 질문 받게 될 수 있으므로 자신의 장점과 경쟁력을 적으면 된다. 중요한 점은 이 본론 부분이 바로 항공사의 키워드와 나의 자질이 조화롭게 만나는 곳으로 좋은 뜻의 단어들만 나열하는 것이 아니라 나만의 단어들로 다른 지원자들과 차별화된 경쟁력을 갖추는 것이 좋다.

5. 마지막 '결론' 부분으로 끝을 맺도록 한다. 마지막 줄 If~로 시작하는 내용에 해당하는 부분으로, 다시 한 번 자신에 대한 어필과 '더 궁금하신 내용은 언제든 연락 바랍니다'라는 내용들을 담고 있다.

Cover Letter 형식에 대한 예시

Applicant's Name

Adress

Company Name

Adress

Dear [Name of person]

어떤 동기로 이력서를 보내게 되었는지에 대한 간략한 설명

본문(간략한 자기소개와 본인 PR)

취업을 희망하는 의지와 각오

끝인사

Yours sincerely,

서명

Full Name

Cover Letter 예문

[Your Address]
[Your contact details]
[Date]

[Employment Address]
Dear [Name of person]

I am writing in response to the advertised vacancy for cabin crew on the internet. The positions seems an ideal prospect in view of my extensive customer service experience. I now desire a fresh challenge, with the opportunity to capitalise on my interest in people, love of travel and flair for serving others.

As my CV reflects, I am currently working as a Sales Assistant at OOO Travel Shop in Sheffield, UK. I assist customer, book tours, help with visual merchandising and handle transactions. The role honed my team-working and customer service skills, increasing my ability to work accurately under presure. Prior to this, I worked as a Sales Supervisor/Visual Merchandiser at OOO Accessories in London. In this busy store, I attended to customers' needs, advising them on products. I also supervised in-store displays, handled complaints and coordinated promotions. the role helped hone my communication and interpersonal skills, increasing my ability to handle difficult customers.

I believe I am a suitable candidate for the position in view of my customer service background and interest in serving people from all cultures. In the meantime, I look forward to hearing from you at your earliest convenience.

Yours sincerely,

HYE JIN LEE

15

Practical Interview for Foreign Airlines

1   Group Discussion

외국 항공사 승무원 그룹 토론에서는 지식보다는 태도를 더 중요하게 평가한다. 토론하는 자세에서 그의 능력이 적나라하게 드러나게 되어 있다. 어떤 경우에도 반박하지 말아야 한다. 오히려 긍정의 실마리를 찾아 긍정해야 한다.

다른 사람이 전혀 엉뚱한 주장을 했다고 해서 "그것은 아닙니다."라는 '말로 제지하는 행동'은 최악이다. 그의 열 마디 가운데 한 가지라도 이해가 가는 부분이 있거든 '~에 대해서는 저도 공감합니다.'라고 말하는 것이 좋다. 그리고 상대의 눈을 쳐다보면서 고개를 끄덕이는 제스처를 해야 한다. 면접관은 그런 사람이 공동체 생활을 잘할 것이라고 판단하게 마련이다. 영어 토론 면접에서는 지원자의 일거수일투족이 모두 체크 대상이다. 토론 팀이 화합을 이룬다면 그 팀은 모두 합격할 가능성이 있다. 팀을 짜서 움직이는 경우 나만 합격한다는 목표로 움직이지 말고 서로 '우리 모두 합격한다'는 목표를 세우고 움직이면 최선의 화음을 만들어 낼 수 있다.

그룹 토론에서 의외로 그룹 전체가 탈락하는 경우도 종종 있다. 주된 이유는 첫 단추를 잘못 뀐 경우가 대부분이다. 예를 들어 처음 시작하는 사람이 주제를 잘못 이해하여 주제와 벗어난 내용을 이야기할 경우 그 사람에게 친절한 태도로 양해를 구한

후 내용을 바로 잡아야 전체 탈락을 방지할 수 있다.

다른 사람들의 이야기를 잘 듣고 구체적으로 어떤 점이 좋은지 칭찬해 준다. 칭찬을 해주면 면접관에게 호의적인 사람으로 비춰질 수 있다. 의견을 말할 때는 앞서 제시된 의견과 연관하여 자신의 의견을 덧붙이는 형식이 독창적인 의견을 제시하는 것보다 수월하며 긍정적인 결과를 갖게 될 가능성이 크다.

토론하는 동안 말을 하지 않고 조용할 경우 면접관은 그 지원자를 지목하여 토론 내용의 요약을 요청하거나 의견들 중 가장 기억에 남는 의견이 무엇인지 물어볼 수 있다. 여기에서 답변을 잘 하면 결과는 거의 합격인 경우가 많으니 너무 당황하지 말도록 하자.

반면에 말을 너무 많이 할 경우(지원자 스스로는 본인의 영어실력이 뛰어나다 생각할 지 모르지만) 남의 이야기를 경청하지 않는 사람으로 비춰질 수 있다. 말이란 많이하는 만큼 실수도 생기게 되고 본의 아니게 다른 지원자들의 발표기회를 뺏을 수 있기 때문이다. 비록 다른 지원자들의 의견이 좋지 않다 하더라도 의견을 적극적으로 경청하는 Good listener 가 되어야 하며 이는 토론에서 가장 중요한 요소임을 명심해야 할 것이다. 팀의 이익을 위해 협조하고 공통의 목표를 향해 갈 수 있는 인재라는 것을 보여주어야 한다.

토론 시 지나치게 튀는 것보다, 상대방의 의견에 귀 기울이고 분위기를 자연스럽게 이끄는 것이 좋다. 이때 중요한 것은 적절한 눈 마주침, 목소리, 반응, 제스처 등이다. 토론 면접의 포인트는 의사소통하고 이해하는데 문제가 없으며 잘 어울려서 팀의 임무를 수행하는데 있다. 토론은 나만 잘 한다고 되는 것이 아니다. 즐겁게 토론하고 팀 분위기도 좋고 주어진 미션을 마치면 팀원 전체가 더 좋은 점수를 받을 수 있다. 전원이 합격하기도 전원이 탈락하기도 하는 것이 토론 면접이다. 그 만큼 팀 분위기가 중요하다.

토론 시 유용한 표현

① 토론 시작

- My name is ⋯ it's great to meet you all.

- Good morning. I'm glad to have a discussion with you.

② 시간 관리

- I'm afraid that we only have 2 minutes left. How about making a conclusion?

- I think it's time for us to finish up. Shall we make a conclusion?

- I think it's a good time for us to arrange our ideas what we have discussed.

- I would like to let you know that we have 5 minutes our of 20 minutes of the discussion time. Shall we sum up?

③ 나의 의견을 제시할 때

- I would like to say that ~

- From my point of view ~

- In my experience(opinion).

- Let me share with you about my personal experience.

- I think we can also think from different point of views. In my opinion, the blind date is⋯

- Why don't we decide a time checker before we start?

④ 동시에 말 시작했을 때

- After you.

- Please go ahead.

- You can go first.

⑤ 의견에 동의할 때

- That is a good point.

- I agree with you on that point.

- I can go along with that idea.

- I follow you with that.

- I second that.

- I agree with you 100%.

- I totally agree with your opinion.

- I was about to say that. I absolutely support your idea because···

- I completely agree to your idea. As you can see···

- I am all for you. I'd like to add something to it.

- That's what I wanted to tell you. As you've mentioned···

- I see what you mean.

- That would be interesting.

- I understand. Let me add to that.

- That's exactly what I mean.

- I (totally) agree with you. Like you said···

- I think your opinion summarizes what I would like to say also.

⑥ 반대할 때(주로 Debate 형식의 토론에 사용할 것)

- I think you have a great idea, but I'm afraid that my opinion is a bit different.
- I am not sure if it is good to ⋯ because~
- I understand why you said about ⋯ but ⋯ regarding ⋯ I am not quite sure it's a good idea to ⋯ because⋯
- I understand your point about ⋯ but I cannot agree with you on ⋯ because⋯

⑦ 상대방에게 지적 또는 반대 의견을 받았을 때

- (I think I misunderstood that.) Thank you for pointing that out.
- It's very nice of you to say that to me. Thank you.
- I didn't know about that. Thank you for correcting me on that.

⑧ 토론의 정리 및 마무리

- So far, we have mentioned about 7 items to be carried when we go to the mountains.
- It's been great talking to you all.
- Nice meeting you all and I hope to see you again soon.
- We have mentioned about 7 items altogether. As we need to select 5 items to be carried to the mountains, shall we make some decisions now? Let's discuss about 2 things that are less important than others.
- I have mentioned about the flashlight and I would like to suggest to remove flashlight as it can be regarded less important than other items that were discussed. What do you think about removing the flashlight?
- I've enjoyed discussing with you.
- I hope we get a good result and see you again soon.
- It was a really good discussion and I learned a lot from you all. Thank you.

 토론의 종류

① 결론 도출형 토론

면접관이 제시한 주제를 어떻게 해결해 나갈지를 의논하는 형태이다. 주어지는 상황은 주로 서비스 관련 직종에 대한 내용들이 많으며 에미레이트 항공에서는 팀으로 무언가를 만드는 team building과 연관한 활동에 관한 것도 있다.

> 예 We are going to have a party, choose 5 celebrities to invite.

② 자유 형식의 토론

하나의 주제에 대해 팀원들이 각자 다른 생각과 의견을 다양하게 나누는 것 뿐만 아니라 상대방의 이야기를 경청하는 것과 그것에 대해 의견을 덧붙여 그렇게 생각하는 이유를 분명하게 설명하는 것이 좋다. 처음보는 다른 지원자들과 얼마나 잘 어울려 대화를 나누는지를 면접관은 주의깊게 관찰할 것이다.

> 예 What are you proud of things about Korean culture?

③ Debate 형식

찬반을 나누어 의견을 제시하고 좋은 점과 그렇지 못한 점에 대해 이야기를 나누는 형태이다.

너무 강한 어조나 상대방의 의견을 무시하는 듯한 태도는 좋지 않다. 나의 의견을 피력하여 상대방을 설득하는 기술도 필요하다.

> 예 Discuss 5 good and bad factor of Korea.

한국에 대해 좋은 점은 쉽게 이야기할 수 있으나 나쁜 점은 쉽지 않다. 이때 보완점과 대책을 함께 제시하면 좋다.

Discussion 기출문제(중동 항공사 기준)

1. What would be the good things and bad things living in Dubai?

2. If you notice your ship is about to sink, which items you would take from your ship. Please name 10 items according to its importance.

a. Beacon	b. Blanket	c. Life jacket
d. Flare	e. Canopy	f. Match
g. 2 gallon of water	h. Compass	i. Purifier Pump
J. Water reservoir	k. Map	l. Mirror
m. Hook knife	n. Chocolate Bar	o. FAK
p. Mobile phone	q. Torch	r. Microphone
s. Waterproof Watch	t. Portable Oxygen	

3. As a manager of 5 star hotel, you can only take 5 customers out of 10 type of customers. Please choose them and clarify the reason accordingly.

   a. kidney patient

   b. customer who already has complain cases

   c. presidential candidate

   d. journalist

   e. the elderly couple who are celebrating their 40th anniversary

   f. Famous party girl

   g. honeymoon couple came from other country

   h. business man who come to attend medical conference

   I. young pregnant lady

   j. well known CEO of major company

   k. the disabled couple

4. You are planning to invite your friends for Christmas party. What kind of food you would like to prepare?

5. What is the difference of transportation system between Korea and other countries?

6. Which 5 items would you like to bring with you when you go travelling?

7. If you go to other planet, what would you like to bring from earth?

   Please list 5 things and reason.

8. If you join for airline, you should live with different nationalities.

   Please choose three nationalities you wish to live with and why.

9. Please list 3 things that you don't like about Koreans.

10. If you have power to change the law, what thing you would like to change?

11. You should arrange 7 days of travel plan, including 4 different nationalities.

    Please decide the entire itinerary for this trip.

12. If I give you one Million dollar, what kind of business you would like to start?

    Please decide type of business, place, and where you would like to donate that profit.

13. Total 20 group tourist will come to Korea for 3days. Please arrange their whole itinerary including, hotel, tourism spots, meals.

14. If you win the lottery, where would you like to donate half of money?

15. What would you choose between fame and fortune?

16. If you are preparing special party for your parents, what kind of party would you like to prepare?

17. If you get an opportunity to change one thing about your country, what would you like to change? How and why?

18. If you start your own company, what would you do for company?

19. If you were to become a recruitment officer, whom would you hire? List 10 qualifications and prioritize them.

20. If doctor says you have only few months to live, how would you alter way of your life?

21. What's the most important thing to choose a man to get marry?

22. What's difference with service in hotel and service in airplane?

23. Discuss the positive and negative aspects of living in Qatar.

24. What would you bring with you if you went to another planet?

25. Good and bad points of Korean people or Korean culture.

26. Choose 10 items that you would take to a deserted island.

27. Choose 5 nationalities of co-workers that you want to live with in the same flat and 5 nationalities of co-workers that you don't want to live with when you live in Qatar.

28. You are about to start a local airline / new restaurant in Dubai and you are on the management team. Create a name for the airline / restaurant, design the uniform, recruitment process and marketing strategy.

29. Choose 3 countries that you would want to live in for the rest of your life and choose the 3countries that you don't want to live in.

2 Essay

일반적으로 약 20분의 시간이 주어지며 A4용지 한 장의 분량을 요구한다. 면접관의 가이드라인은 아주 중요하다. 그것을 놓치면 룰을 지키지 않는 사람으로 평가되어 불합격할 수 있으니 주의하도록 하자. 예를 들어 면접관이 Time's up! 이라고 하면 비록 에세이 결론을 내지 못하였더라도 펜을 내려놓아야 한다. 완성하지 못했다고 불합격 되지는 않으나 가이드라인을 어기면 불합격 된다. 간혹 지원자가 쓴 에세이를 가지고 최종 면접때 다시 묻기도 한다. 그러므로 에세이는 반드시 긍정적인 내용으로 작성하고 내가 어떤 이야기를 썼는지도 기억하고 있어야 한다.

주제를 받게 되면 맨 처음 할 일은 마인드 맵을 그려 주제와 연관된 단어나 생각을 간단하게 메모한 후 이를 토대로 에세이를 작성하면 비교적 빠른 시간 안에 일관성 있게 써내려 갈 수 있다.

먼저 에세이의 제목을 읽어보고 구상을 해보고 형태는 서론, 본론, 결론의 명확한 구조를 잡도록 한다. 가장 보편적인 형태가 5절인데 첫째 절을 서론으로 둘, 셋, 네 번째 절은 본문, 그리고 마지막 5번째 절을 결론으로 한다.

너무 많은 형용사나 부사 등의 사용은 피하고 같은 단어를 되풀이해서 사용하지 않도록 하고 속어나 약어를 피해야하며 스펠링 확인은 반드시 한 후 쓴 글의 행과 행 운 더블 스페이스를 두고 오자를 화이트로 수정하지 않도록 한다.

① 서론(Introduction Paragraph)

서두와 마무리는 가장 중요한 역할이며 자신의 주장만을 단순하게 말한다면 다른 에세이와 차별화를 둘 수 없는 평범한 작품이 되어버린다. 가장 일반적인 방법은 6하 원칙 중 1-2로 시작하는 방법이다. 이때 중요한 것은 에세이를 읽는 상대방이 그 에세이에서 무엇을 기대해도 되는지에 대한 기본적인 개념을 전달해야 하는 것이다. 따라서 자신이 그 에세이에서 정작하고자 하는 말이 무엇인지를 요약해 표현하는 방법이 가장 일반적이라고 본다.

② 본론(Support Paragraph)

주장을 뒷받침하는 내용들로 증거들을 제시한다. 추상적인 내용보다는 좀 더 구체적이고 실질적인 예들을 보여주도록 한다.

- Listing different point : First / Second / Third
- Counter example : However / Even though / On the other hand
- Additional ideas : Another / In addition to / Furthermore
- To show cause and effect : Therefore / As a result / Consequently

③ 결론(Summary Paragraph)

결론부의 마지막 한 두 문장에서는 자신의 주장과 생각을 반드시 명시해야 한다. 기억에 남을만한 에세이가 되기 위해선 자신이 하고자 하는 말의 요점을 정리하며 결론짓는 것이다. 서두에서 명확하지 않는 주장이나 생각을 펼쳤다면 결론부에서 다시 한 번 그 부분을 확실히 해주는 것이 필요하다.

④ Essay example

Kimchi is a korean traditional food, and Koreans have eaten Kimchi for a long time ago. In addition it is a fact well known to the world that Kimchi has beneficial effects.

First, Kimchi contains a lot of vitamins, and the vitamins help the activation of physical metabolism in the human body. Also, it keeps the balance of nutrition.

secondly, Another efficacy of Kimchi that it is a low calorie food that vegetables as a subject. It contains a lot of dietary fiber and lowers sugar and cholesterol, so it helps the prevention of geriatric diseases such as glycosuria, heart disease, and obesity.

Lastly, Kimchi is a fermentation food so that it contains a lot of lactobacillus. it helps to keep a stomach and intestine strong.

To sum up, eating Kimchi has a lot of benefits. Whoever concern about their health, it is must food you should try. Where on earth you will be able to find such food that has full of nutrition and even helps for a diet. I strongly believe that it is one of best food in the world.

Essay 작성 시 문장을 시작하는 구문 예시

- For such reason : 그런 이유로~

- Plus : 또한

- Furthermore = Moreover : 더욱이, 게다가

- In addition to that : 더 나아가

- Therefore : 그러므로

- Consequently = Hence : 따라서

- To sum up : 요약하자면

- Finally = As it turns out = Eventually : 결과적으로

- Looking back : ~예전에는(과거의 예를 들 때)

- Once : ~한 번은(어떤 예를 들 때)

- More importantly : 더 중요한건

- Since that : 그렇기 때문에

- Whereas = On the other hand : 반면에

- Surprisingly : 놀랍게도

- Similarly = In that way : 이와 같이, 이와 비슷하게

- First and foremost : 무엇보다 먼저, 일단은

- By and large = all in all : 대체로는

- In my view = From my stand point = From my prospective : 내 생각
  에는

- The main reason is that : 주된 이유는

- To be specific : 더 자세히 얘기하자면

- To begin with : 우선, 먼저

- Generally speaking = broadly speaking : 일반적으로, 대체로 말하면

- Roughly speaking : 대략적으로 말하자면, 간단히 말하자면

- In line with that = in association with that : 이처럼, 이와 같이

- I think highly of ~ = ~ is what I do value the most
  ~을 중요시하다. 중요하게 생각한다.
  예 Having various experiences are what I do value the most.
     I think highly of having good relationships with people around me.

- pros and cons : 찬성과 반대, 장점과 단점
  예 The pros and cons of school uniforms continues to be a hot topic.

- In an effort to ~ = In an attempt to ~

  ~을 하기 위해서, 노력의 일환으로

  > In an effort to provide a good service to my customers,
  >
  > In an effort to achieve my goal,
  >
  > In an attempt to become a cabin crew,

- in favor of ~ing : ~하는데 찬성이다

  > I'm in favor of studying abroad.

- Not to mention = Needless to say = It is not too much to say = There is no doubt that = I can confidently say that = I am convinced that 의심할 나위 없이, 확실히 말하자면

⑤ Essay Subject

1. Why do people kill for money?

2. What's your competitive advantage over other applicant?

3. The most embarrassed moment in your life.

4. Out of 10 points, how many points would you give to yourself and why?

5. What is the most important character as a cabin crew?

6. Do we need censorship on the internet?

7. What's the biggest mistake in your life? How did you overcome?

8. Tell me what you have lucky or unlucky in your life?

9. If you have a chance to change about your life, what would you like to do?

10. Why are there more female than male flight attendant?

11. What is your important event in your life?

12. Write a letter for an recruitment manager for our company.

13. Tell me about blood donation.

14. Do you function best in the morning, afternoon, or evening?

15. If your doctor told you that you had only few months to live, how would you alter your way or life?

16. Which of four seasons of the year appeals to you the most?

17. Would you want to live in large city or not?

18. What is the best advice you ever got?

19. What situation is most stressful for you?

20. Why do you think time management is so important?

21. What was the most important lesson that you have learned in your life?

22. Tell me about your complex.

23. What is the best service?

24. If a foreign friend comes to Korea, where would you like to go together?

25. Some people choose flatmate who are from different country, other people prefer same nationality. Who do you prefer?

26. What would be the advantage and disadvantage of living in multi-cultural country?

3 Partner Introduction

파트너 소개는 처음 만난 사람과 얼마나 오픈 마인드로 대화하며 친해질 수 있는 지를 평가할 수 있는 면접 형태이다. 아울러 상대방 소개를 하면서 이야기 하는 당사 자의 긍정적 혹은 부정적인 성격이 드러나기도 한다.

주제가 정해진다면 보통 스포츠, 음악, 영화, 음식, 여행 등 취미에 관련된 소재가 대부분이다. 주제가 정해지지 않고 서로를 소개하라고 한다면 가장 인상적인 부분이 나 좋은 내용만을 면접관에게 말해야 하며 파트너의 단점이 드러나는 이야기는 빼야 한다. 파트너 소개는 파트너에 대한 평가가 아니라 나를 위한 평가의 기초라는 것을 명심하도록 하자. 대화하는 동안 상대방에게 경청하고, 파트너의 영어 실력에 맞게 궁금한 점은 적극적으로 질문을 하여 알아내도록 하자. 파트너 소개는 결국 자기소 개라고 생각하며 장점을 부각시켜주고 칭찬을 많이 하도록 하는 것이 좋다.

Partner를 소개할 때의 주안점

- Favorite destination of favorite airlines

- Favorite traveling spot

- Favorite food and restaurant

- Worst dating episode

- Favorite …

- Favorite book, souvenir

- Favorite movies, color, animal

 Partner 소개의 유의사항

- 상대방의 말을 repeat 하지 말자.
- 포인트 되는 말
- 가능하면 재미있게 하자.
- 표정과 eye contact 유의하자.

① 유머가 있는 경우

It was really short time talking with her but I can still catch her sense of humor. Actually humor is something always best way to break the ice and feel intimacy. So, it was really short time though, but now I feel much closer thanks to my partner.

② 편안함을 주는 경우

Actually, we're trying but it's really easy to feel comfortable here but I think I'm luck to meet my partner cause she make me laugh and feel comfortable. There in no doubt this is something show who she is.

③ 첫인상을 가지고 이야기하는 경우

If you see my partner, you would easily find what is my partner's attractive point is. She got a really beautiful (special) _____. When she talk with that _____, I can feel she is really attractive person. I hope everyone can catch this and find her value.

④ 배우고자 하는 점이 있는 경우

It was kind of amazing for me to hear her dynamic experiences. Through her story, I'm interested in ~~~ She let me know experience is always the best teacher. She let me know sharing of other's life story can inspire and change other's life as well. It was really great to talk to her.

4 Picture Description Activity

그림에 대해 있는 그대로 묘사를 하라고 하는 경우 일반적으로 생각을 배제한 fact 만을 얘기해야 한다. 상대방이 지원자의 묘사를 듣고 비슷하게라도 그 그림을 그릴 수 있을 정도면 완벽하다. 우선 사진에 보이는 것을 주된 사람이나 사물부터 묘사하도록 하고, 동작이나 행동을 이야기할 때에는 현재 시제나 현재 진행형 시제를 사용한다.

하지만 면접관에 따라 스토리텔링을 요구하거나 그림 다음에 어떤 일이 일어날지 질문을 하기도 한다. 지원자가 평소 긍정적이고 오픈 마인드를 가진 사람이라면 보여지는 그림에 대해 밝고 즐거운 내용으로 스토리텔링할 것이고, 그렇지 않은 사람이라면 그림의 부정적인 내용을 말하게 된다. 즉 설명하는 내용에 따라 지원자의 성향을 알 수 있는 단서가 된다는 것을 명심하자.

그림 묘사 연습

5 Article Summary

단락 요약은 면접관이 건네주는 A4용지 반 정도의 분량을 소리내어 읽고 내용을 요약하는 면접이다. 정확한 발음으로 읽고, 읽는 동안 핵심 포인트를 파악한 뒤 요약 하도록 한다. 내용을 요약할 때는 이해된 내용을 자신만의 단어로 쉽고 간단하게 설 명하는 것이 포인트다. 추측성 발언은 금물이고 동문서답하여서도 아니 되며, 이해가 잘 되지 않았을 경우 면접관에게 양해를 구한 후 다시 한 번 읽어도 된다. 읽을 때의 모습과 자세도 중요하니 종이로 입을 가리지 않도록 주의하면서 큰 목소리로 또박또 박 읽는다. 약간의 미소를 지으며 읽는 연습을 해보도록 하자.

지원하는 항공사의 최신 뉴스나 항공사 관련 소식들을 읽고 요약해보는 연습을 하 도록 한다. 주어지는 Article에 항공서비스 지식이나 항공 전문 용어 등이 나오기도 하므로 항공용어를 미리 공부해두면 도움이 된다.

 ## Article 요약 실전 연습

1. In-seat telephone

Use the satellite telephone in every seat to call any phone in the world at only US$5 per minute. All major credit cards are accepted, as well as pre-paid telephone cards (available onboard). You can also use the phone to speak to someone seated elsewhere on board.

Summary :

193

2. Scandinavian airline SAS announced a massive overhaul of the company. A Scandinavian airline SAS MD-80 and Boeing 737 aircraft parked at the gates at terminal 4 at Arlanda Airport north of Stockholm, 03 February 2009. Scandinavian airline group SAS AB on 03 February 2009 announced a massive overhaul of the company. The struggling company said it would reduce its staff from 23,000 to 14,000, mostly by selling subsidiary airlines but also by laying off 3,000 SAS employees.

◎ Summary :

3. Those traveling to U.S. destinations aboard Asiana Airlines between December 1 and January 15 totaled 98,321 passengers, jumping 10.1 percent from the same period a year ago. The average occupancy rate for U.S. routes posted 87.3 percent, up 4.3 percentage points from the previous year. In particular, the ratio of foreigners increased approximately 15 percentage points.

◎ Summary :

4. Korean Air disclosed that the number of passengers aboard Korean Air routes to the U.S. in December last year marked 187,000 passengers, rising 7 percent from the same period a year ago. The number of passengers who booked flights in January also increased 7 percent from the same period last year.

◎ Summary :

5. Emirates Airlines will deploy Airbus A380 carriers on its Incheon-Dubai route from November, the company announced yesterday. This will be the first time the Airbus A380 is used in commercial flights not only to Korea but Northeast Asia, the company said. The Dubai-based carrier currently operates A380 carriers on Dubai-New York and Dubai-London routes and plans to introduce A380 carriers to its Dubai-Sydney-Oakland route early this year. The carriers are equipped with shower facilities, bar and lounge for first and business class passengers, seats equipped with massage functions and onboard entertainment system with over 1,000 channels, the company said.

◎ Summary :

6. Whether they're flying alone or with their families, we make sure our youngest travellers receive the utmost care and attention. The special treatment begins the moment you contact us to make a reservation and continues throughout the entire flight experience. We offer separate check-in facilities for young passengers travelling alone, and dedicated Emirates staff members to accompany them to and from the aircraft. We also provide priority boarding for families with young children, and every plane is equipped with changing tables and bassinets for your comfort and convenience.

Summary:

7. While you're booking travel, why not arrange for an airport transfer to or from your doorstep? Complimentary chauffeur-driven cars are available for our First and Business Class passengers in many of the cities we serve. You can make all the arrangements online during the booking process, and then set your mind at ease—it's one less thing to worry about during your travels.

Summary:

Summary 답변 예시

1. This article is explaining a wide range of channels and games offered on Emirates flights for a pax entertainment. For its contents, there are Live BBC, radio, music, video games, including latest movies.

2. SAS announced massive overhaul of the company. In line with that, they decided to reduce number of staffs from its subsidiary airlines and by lay off.

3. Asiana declared its pax glows specially for US routes. It mainly caused by increasement of foreign pax.

4. Korean Air announced 7 percent of pax glows compare with last year. Also, January alone showed same number of increasement rate.

5. Emirates Airlines will deploy A380 for Dubai-Incheon flight, as a forth destination but the first for the northeast Asia. It is equipped with various functions for the comfort of passengers on board.

6. Emirates offers the utmost service to young pax by special check in counter and exclusive companion staff to and form aircraft for travelling alone and priority boarding for family with young pax.

7. Airlines offers complimentary airport transportation service for first and business pax. Pax can make arrangement online when they book.

6 Written Test

Sign, Notice 등은 중동항공사 필기시험에서 출제 빈도가 가장 높으며 때때로 1차 면접 시에도 나오기도 한다. 아래의 문제들은 항공 산업에 종사하고 있다면 반드시 알아야 할 중요한 문제들은 모아 보았다. 의외로 헷갈릴 수 있으니 문제를 풀어본 뒤 꼭 숙지해야 할 것이다.

이 외에도 간단한 문법문제, 독해, 그리고 시차에 관련된 문제풀기 등이 필기시험에 주로 나온다.

Look at the signs / notice below. Someone ask you what each sign /notice means. Mark your answers on the answer sheet.

1. TWO TABLETS TO BE TAKEN THREE TIMES A DAY

   A. Take one tablets a day

   B. Take five tablets a day

   C. Take six tablets a day

   D. Take nine tablets a day

2. KEEP OUT OF REACH OF CHILDREN

   A. Let children touch this item

   B. This item is dangerous to children

   C. Children should not reach this item

   D. Children keep on reaching this item

3. NO ENTRY TO UNAUTHORIZED PERSONS

A. Always make sure you see the clerk before you leave the place.

B. Don't wait in this area

C. Make sure you go into the room by yourself

D. Only authorized persons can enter this area

4. NO ANIMALS IN RESIDENTIAL FACILITIES

A. Residents are not permitted to have pets

B. Facilities are prepared for animals.

C. Animals can be dangerous in this place

D. Residential areas are among animals

5. THIS PLACE IS OFF-LIMITS TO STUDENTS

A. Only teachers have limited places to rest.

B. This place is out-of-bounds for students

C. The boundary of this area is too wide for students

D. You should call in a limited time.

6. EMERGENCY EXIT / KEEP CLEAR AT ALL TIMES

A. Never stand or leave things in front of this door.

B. No adult are allowed.

C. Do not open the door in case of emergency

D. The door must be kept unlocked.

7. WE REGRET WE CANNOT ACCEPT PAYMENT BY CASH

A. If you spend much, you have to pay by credit card.

B. We make a charge if you pay credit card.

C. You cannot pay by cash.

D. We prefer cash payment for large sales.

8. ENGLISH TUTOR FOR HIRE

A. English Institute is seeking for a tutor.

B. Hiring process is done for English tutors.

C. Tutor are ready for studying English.

D. An English tutor is seeking for job.

9. MAKE TAX CUTS PERMANENT FOR HYBRID CAR BUYERS

A. Car sellers should be protected in many ways.

B. Customers who purchase hybrid cars will pay reduced tax.

C. Hybrid cars are available to many car buyers.

D. Tax policy is changing for hybrid car plants.

10. MICROSOFT TO CUT COSTS.

A. Microsoft will reduce spending money.

B. Microsoft habe cut cost since last year.

C. Cost is nit high in Microsoft.

D. Cost will be rising in Microsoft.

11. ABC AIRWAYS SIGNS DEAL FOR A350S

A. ABC Airways plans to purchase 80 aircraft.

B. ABC Airways made a deal with 80 customers on A350.

C. ABC Airways signs are dealt with A350s.

D. Dealing A350 is not easy for ABC Airways.

Chapter 4

외국항공사 면접전형
/ 항공사별 기출문제

Airline
English
Interview

2018-2019년 기준 에미레이트 항공 면접 전형

최근 에미레이트 항공 승무원 채용시 두가지 형태로 채용이 되고 있다.

매달 세계 여러 도시에서 오픈데이가 열리며, 온라인 지원 없이 준비 서류를 들고 직접 면접에 참가하는 방식이 첫 번째이고, 또다른 방식은 어세스먼트 데이로 온라인 지원을 한 후 'Shortlisted' 된 지원자에 한해 파이널 전 단계인 다음 절차 CV Drop부터 그룹 면접까지 참가 할 수 있다.

 ## 오픈데이

- 서류 및 사진 등 필수 준비 사항들 준비하여 직접 참가
- CV Drop → 그룹 면접 → 1:1 화상 면접

① CV Drop

② Group Discussion 1

20명 정도가 한 조가 되어 주어진 시간 내에 토론하기.(그림 묘사, 워드 슈팅)

③ Group Discussion 2

10명 정도가 한 조가 되어 주어진 시간 내에 주재에 대해 토론하기

● Group discussion 1

Discuss about the Pucture 1 together -〉 Each person have to present to the assessor

🔲 How to use this item

🔲 Talk about 3things about this city

In this assessment, you will be placed in groups, generally of two.

(Exemple 1)

You will receive a card with a picture of a city on it and you have to discuss this city with your partner.

You can use any means to get more information on the city and after 10 minutes you will have to present three things in the city to the assessors.

● Group Discussion 2

Over booking situation

You are a manager

Hotel, Cruise, Airline, Rental company etc

(Example 1)

You are 12 people on a sinking ship.

There is an escape boat, however, only eight people fit in it. Your group has to discuss who will be saved. You have 15 minutes to come up with a unanimous decision.

(Example 2)

Your ship makes an emergency landing on the moon. You have the following equipment with you:

Flashlight

Parachute

Water

Compass

etc

Chose three priority items that you would take with you from the ship. When your group has reached consensus, write them down on the white-board. You have 15 minutes to complete the task.

Example 3

You have the following group of cabin crew:

Yusuki – 22 – Japan – smoker

Maria – 24 – US – smoker

Anna – 29 – Kenya – non-smoker

Iman – 27 – Morocco – non-smoker

Sofia – 25 – Egypt – smoker

Yen – 22 – China – non-smoker

Your group is the airline's accommodation department that decides which cabin crew get paired up in 2 bedroom apartments. You will present your decision and explain your criteria for selection in 15 minutes.

Example 4

You are working the London-Dubai sector, and you have the following complaints in the aircraft:

1A – Mr. Smith – frequent traveler complains that he did not get a seat with leg room

10 C – Mrs. Jones traveling with a child and an infant did not receive a toy for her child

12H - Mr. Rogers TV doesn't work

14K - Mr. Ford did not get his diabetic meal.

What is your order of priorities in solving these complaints and what solutions would you offer.

The group has 20 minutes to decide.

Exemple5

It's an over booking situation.

You are a owner of the car rental company.

There are 6 customers want to rent a car but only 3cars available.

And all customers have difficult situation, they all need to rent a car.

Which customer would you like to give a deal?

You can choose 3 customers and explain why you choose them and why you don't choose rest of them.

Share your opinion and make a conclusion with other members.

The group has 10mins to make a conclusion.

④ 1:1 화상 면접

1:1 화상 면접으로 약 40분 이상 소요되며, 일경험 바탕 질문들 위주로 물어 보며, 답한 내용에 대해 꼬리 질문 형식으로 진행, 팀워크, 동료와의 관계, 피드백, 고객관련, 어려웠던 경험등 이력서 바탕으로 일경험에 관련한 여러 질문들을 한다.

화상 면접 또한 실제 면접과 같이 사람이 면접을 보기 때문에, 렌즈를 보며 밝은 표정, 바른 자세 유지하며, 인사하는것 또한 잊지 말자.

어세스먼트 데이

- 온라인 접수 → 그룹 면접 → 1:1 화상 면접
- 그룹면접은 위 오픈데이와 동일

Final 기출문제

- Whats your current job?

- Whats your duties?

- Have you ever received or gave feedback to your co-worker?

- Tell me your busiest day at work?

- Have you made an excellent team work?

- Describe a stressful event in your life and how you dealt with it.

- Have you ever had to deal with a difficult customer? How did you do so?

- Why nationalities do you think you will have the most difficulty dealing with?

- Tell me about a time when you had to make a difficult decision.

- What was the worst mistake you have ever made?

- What do you know about Dubai?

- What do you know about Emirates Airlines?

- Tell me what do you do? (Your current job and what's your roles)

- You've worked in __, how was it?

- Have you met a demanding customer? How did you handle?

- Have you provided best service so the customer was very happy about your service

- Have you made good relationship with your co-worker?

- Have you ever gave feedback to your co-worker? (Good or Bad)

그 외 자주 등장하는 Final Questions 25

1. Tell me about yourself

2. Why do you want to work for our airline?

3. Tell me about your career goal

4. Do you work better in a team or alone?

5. How would your friends or coworkers describe you?

6. Tell me about a time when you helped someone.

7. Tell me about a time you made a suggestion to improve business.

8. Tell me about the most fun you ever experienced on the job.

9. What are your strengths?

10. What are your weaknesses?

11. Tell me about a time when you had to deal with a co-worker who wasn't doing his/her fair share of the work. What did you do and what was the outcome

12. Tell me about a time you misjudged a person.

13. Tell me about a challenge at work you faced and overcame recently.

14. Tell me about a time you resolved a conflict.

15. Have you worked with someone you didn't like? If so, how did you handle it?

16. Would you say that you can easily deal with high-pressure situations?

17. What do you expect from a supervisor?

18. What motivates you to do the best on the job?

19. What is the kind of person you refuse to work with?

20. How long do you expect to work for us if hired?

21. What did you do to prepare for this interview?

22. Are you applying for any other airlines? What if more than one airline offers you the job?

23. Why should we hire you?

24. Do you have any questions for me?

 ## 카타르 면접 절차 (2018년도부터 2019 4월)

① CV Drop

- 아주 짧은 시간내에 간단한 Small Talk. 대화형식의 이력서 바탕 기본 질문들

  예 면접관 : Good morning, Nice to see you!

  지원자 : Good morning, My name is ____This is my CV

로 시작하면서

What is your applicant number?

What do you do?

How long have you been working?

Have you lived in __?

Tell me your experiences in __that you've learned/achieved

중점전략포인트!

- 국제적 매너, 인사
- 다가가는 태도와 자세
- 외적 이미지
- 적극적 자세, 마인드
- 활짝 웃는 호감가는 인상, 그루밍 상태
- 영어 회화 실력

　기본 질문 외 최근 당황 할수 있는 질문들을 여러가지 주로 물어 보면서 파악하고 있으며, 당황 할수 있는 질문에도 밝은 미소를 잃지 않고 긍정적이고 적극적인 자세와 호감을 줄수 있는 국제적 매너로 임한다면 CV Drop에서 좋은 결과를 갖게 될 것이다.

　CV Drop에서는 기본적으로 원활히 소통 할수있는 스피킹 실력을 갖추어야 하며, 실제 면접에서는 영어 실력 자체 보다 호감가는 이미지, 밝은 표정, 자세, 성격적인면에 더 초점을 두므로, 평소에도 웃는 연습을 많이 하면서 긍정적인 마인드를 갖추도록 하자.

예 Q : What do you think of unhealthy food?

Q : What do you think of authority?

Q : What do you think of natural digesters?

② 다음날

암리치 :212cm 이상

스카, 문신 체크 하면서 워드 슈팅, 센텐스 슈팅 과 뜻밖의 생소한 질문들을 여러가지 물어본다. 암리치 안되는 탈락자는 바로 퇴장

"Sentence Shooting"은 질문지 스스로 뽑고 답변하기 방식

예 Q : What was the most regrettable thing that you couldn't do it in the past?

Q : What do you think of adopting a pet?

위 면접절차에서 합격하여 호명 되시면 다음 절차 진행

③ Public Speaking : 그림묘사

그림 (사물 하나)를 2명이 한조를 이루어 한사람은 그림 그대로 묘사 하고 'In Original Way' 다른 파트너는 'In Creative Way' 하게 묘사 설명 하기

예 가위, 재봉틀(카타르는 그룹 디스커션은 생략되기도 함)

④ 위 면접에 다 통과 되면 최종면접에 초대

파이널에서는 특히 대거 채용 시 되도록이면 모두 채용을 해가려고 하기 때문에 질문에 대한 답변을 할때 미소를 잃지 않고, 당황하지 않으며 확신을 갖고 확고한 의지로 답변을 한다면 좋은 결과가 있을 것이다.

파이널 합격 후에도 피부 상태 또는 치아 문제로 사진을 따로 요청하기도 하는데, 평소에 피부 관리도 잘 하면서 좋은 상태로 면접에 임하도록 하자.

소요시간 : 약 20분

Yes / No 질문들

- 질문에 대해 Yes or No 한후 답변 하기
- 인적성 파악 관련 문제들 : 긍정적인 답변으로 승무원직 수행에 대한 확신을 주어야 함

최근 파이널 기출 문제

Q : Have you served alcohol drinks to customers?

Q : Have you provided a service to customers?

Q : How do you think about the word "Change"?, do you have a positive opinion or negative opinion?

Q : Are you willing to commit in the aviation industry?

Q : Will you acknowledge the guests when you are busy?

Q : Are you a person who acts first or the person who monitor first then act?

Q : When you need some helps, will you ask? Give me an example.

2018년도 루프트한자 면접 절차 및 내용

- 채용 : 20명 가량

루프트한자 1차 면접

- 면접장소 : 한국 산업인력공단
- 이틀간 진행 : 면접날짜와 시간을 선택 가능
- 면접관 2명 : 현직 루프트한자 승무원, 캐빈크루 독일 매니저
- 한조 7명 / 각 조 면접 시간 : 약 30분(개인의 이름과 번호 네임택 건네줌)

- ✓ 대기장소에 가기전 출석 체크
- ✓ 키 160cm 넘는지 체크
- ✓ 앞 타임 면접이 끝날 때까지 대기

① 한국인 면접관

- 질문지를 펴서 먼저 읽고 몇 초 생각 후 답

② 개인들이 뽑은 것을 말하고 답하기

예 Q : 너를 꽃에 비유해봐

Q : 우리 회사에 대해 안 좋은 점

Q : Can you imagine a life without smart phones? Tell us good things and bad things

- 생각 후 답하기

③ 기내 방송문 읽기

- 영어와 한국어중 선택해서 읽기

파이널

- 장소 : K-move 해외취업센터

- 3일에 걸쳐서 면접 진행

- 면접관 : 독일 캐빈크루 매니저, 현직 한국인 승무원

- 모두 영어로 진행, 마지막에 몇 개만 한국어로 질문

- 루프트한자에 입사 확정이 될 경우 이것저것 서류 준비와 관련된 내용, 복지(하우징 이나 월급), 정보제공동의서 등 작성, 범죄경력증명서의 사본 제출

파이널 기출

Q : 자기소개 후 자기소개 에 대한 꼬리 질문

Q : Whats your weakness

Q : What are the differences between German passengers and Korean passengers do you think?

Q : (한국어질문) 왜 한국 항공사 아니고 외국항공사를 가고 싶으신가요?

Q : (한국어 롤플레잉) 비빔밥을 원하는 손님 (외국에서 오래 사셔서 한식을 드시고 싶어하심), 근데 비빔밥이 없는 상황.

- 면접 마친후 수영 가능 여부, 타투 여부 질문

전략포인트!

- 자연 스러운 이미지와 밝고 솔직한 성격
- 루밍 : 본인에게 가장 잘 어울리게
- 면접 복장 : 차분하게 어필 할수 있는 블루 계열 선호

 케세이 항공 2019년 한국인 채용 면접 절차

 2019년 케세이 퍼시픽 한국인 승무원 채용 비디오 기출 문제

1. 한국에 방문하면 해야 할 액티비티는?

2. 너의 직원이 와인쏟았다. 고객이 매우 화가 나있다. 어떻게 대처할거니?

1. 너가 놀이공원 감독인데 동료가 이 지역사람도 아닌 관광객에게 프리패스 티켓을 줘서 다른 고객들이 불공평하다고 컴플레인을 했다. 어떻게 할래?

2. K-pop이 왜 인기라고 생각하는가?

1. 호텔 VIP 손님이 생일날이라고 업그레이드 요청, 어떻게 할래?

2. Why do you think that you are qualified/fit for the cabin crew position?

1. 서울을 처음 방문하는 여행객에게 must-do activity 추천하기

2. 도서관 사서인데 한 고객이 어린이 코너의 아이들이 시끄럽다고 컴플레인 한다. 어떻게 할 것인가?

1. 슈퍼에서 일하는데 손님이 유통기한이 지난 물건을 보고 SNS에 올린다고 했다. 너는 어떻게 대처할 것인가

2. 호텔에서 VIP 손님이 생일이라고 룸을 업그레이드 해달라고 한다. 어떻게 할 것인가

① **온라인 접수**

② **비디오인터뷰:HireVue**

- 비디오 인터뷰 기출 문제 두문제로 구성

③ **파이널 인터뷰**

파이널 면접 내용/절차

1. 암리치 측정 (208cm)

2. 한국어 아티클 또는 기내문 읽기

3. 준비된 서류 제출

④ **1:1 Q/A**

- 개인 신상 기본 질문, 지원동기
- 이력서 바탕 일경험 질문
- 꼬리, 압박 질문 위주와 롤플레이
- 영문 아티클 리딩후 요약/느낀점 말하기
- 한국인 면접관이 한국어 인터뷰 진행, 홍콩 면접관이 영어로 진행
- 압박, 꼬리 질문들을 받았을때 당황 할수도 있는 질문들도 있어 보였고, 당황 할수 있는 롤플레이 질문들도 주었지만, 일경험 바탕의 꼬리, 압박 질문 형태의 면접 진행

  예 Q : 기억나는 손님 말해봐
  ~~~ 그래서

217

그럼 손님 맞이 해서 그렇게 대처 했어

그럼 "~~ 다면 어떻게 했을 건데?"

(다른 상황 제시)

답변내용 스토리속의 다른 상황을 던져주고 롤플레이 압박 꼬리

"이 상황이면 넌 어떻게 할거야?"

라는 문제,

기내 일반 롤플레이 문제들과

고객의 컴플레인 상황 롤플레이 질문들이

많이 다루어짐

예
- 케세이퍼시픽은 왜 지원했어?
- 여기서 얻고싶은게 뭐야?
- 이번 채용서 떨어 진다면?
- 왜 떨어 졌다고 생각해?
- 케세이퍼시픽 타본적 있어?
- 왜 국내항공사에 지원안했어?
- 해외 경험
- 거기서 얻은게 뭐야?

롤플레이 예
- How would you handle, if one of your co-workers was not willing to work?
- No more blankets in the cabin : What would you do?
- No meal choice
- Upset customer

⑤ 메디컬

하이난항공

기존 면접 절차

1. 서류
2. 1차 면접(그룹디스커션)
3. 2차 면접
4. 신체검사
5. 최종합격

모든 면접은
다른 외항사들과 마찬가지로
영어로 시작해서
파이널도 영어로 진행하며,
중국어 능력은 필수 자격 사항이 아닙니다.
당연히 제2외국어 가능 하면
플러스 자격 조건이 됨.

중국계 항공사에선
그루밍, 스킨, 스카 체크를 엄격히 하는 편이므로 상처, 문신이 없어야 하며, 피부
관리에 신경 많이 쓰시는게 좋다. 전체적으로 영어 면접 질문의 난이도는 까다롭고
할 수 있는 꼬리 질문 위주 보다 기본 질문들 많이 물어보기에 다소 쉬운 편이다. 모
든 면접은 영어로 진행, 중국어 가능자는 중국어로 간단한 질문 주고 받기도 한다.

1차 면접

"스탠딩 면접"
10명이 한조가 되어 서서 롤플레이 주제로 그룹 디스커션이 진행

파이널 에서도 10명이 한조가 되어

개별 질문들 나가고, "Prompt Speech" (즉흥 스피치) 가 있다.

"Prompt Speech"는 뽑은 질문지에 대해 30초 안으로 스피치

합격후 트레이닝

• 3개월 동안 실시
• 하이난의 성도 하이코우에서 2개월
• 본사가 위치한 베이징에서 1개월 받고 비행 시작

 ## 2018년도 채용 기준-동방항공 면접 절차

• 서류제출 서류전형 - 1차면접 - 2차면접 - 최종면접 신체 검사

1차 면접

• 한국어 면접 / 면접관 :여자 승무원 4명
• 6명이 한조가 되서 면접 진행되고 개별 질문을 한다.

기출문제

• 본인의 외적, 내적 장점은?
• 동방항공 승무원이 된다면, 어떤 능력을 발휘할 수 있는가?
• 중국어는 얼마나 배웠나?

2차 면접

• 영어로 진행 면접관 여승무원 5명,부지사장
• 기내문 읽기(중국어 또는 영어)
• 영어 개별 질문
• 중국어로도 물어봄

3차 면접

- 5명이 한조가 되어 면접 진행/본사 면접관 4명, 부지사장
- 이력서 바탕으로 중궁어로 개별 질문, 영어 개별 질문
- 취미,중국생활, 중국에 대해.전공 등 기본 질문

4차 면접

- 7명 이 한조가 되어 면접 진행
- 워킹 테스트 : 두바퀴 돌기
- 기본적 질문과 롤플레이

외항사 면접 성공 스토리

 2018년 카타르 부산 채용 후기1

CV DROP (2018.2.16)

제가 받은 질문은 Teamwork 어떻게 생각하니? 현재 뭐하니? 였어요.

두 질문 다 연습했던 질문들이라 무난하게 답했어요. 사실 2번째 질문에서는 답을 하려고 할 때 면접관님께서 이미 인비를 적고 계셨습니다!

ASSESSMENT DAY (2월 17일)

어세스먼트 데이 날도 인원 수가 너무 많아 2월 17일 오전, 오후 2월 18일 오전 이렇게 3조로 나눠졌는데 저는 2월 17일 오전조 였어요

카타르 프레젠테이션을 보고 영어테스트를 진행했어요. 토익 수준으로 그냥 무난하게 봤던 것 같아요 저희 조에서는 10분정도 떨어지셨어요. 그 후에, 1~75번까지는 마리아, 아니타 조. 76~149(?)번까지는 아가, 티나 조였어요

두 조로 나뉘어서 암리치를 하고 스카 체크, 바로 스몰톡(=센텐스 슈팅)에 들어갔어요. 저는 질문에 Are you artistic person?과 세가지 사항 중 뭐가 제일 중요하니였어요. 스몰톡까지 끝나고 합격 번호를 불러 제 번호가 있었고, 퍼블릭 스피치를 시작했어요.

저와 파트너 한명이 랜덤 카드를 뽑아 그 사물을 한명은 original way, 나머지 한명은 creative way로 설명을 해야하는데 저랑 제 파트너는 "가위"를 뽑았고 저는 original way를 설명했어요.

통과된 후, 파이널은 딜레이가 될 것 같다면서 저희한테 일괄적으로 메일을 주신다고 하셨어요.

제가 답하는 모든 질문 하나하나에 Why? How? Tell me your experiene 또는 For example을 물어보셨어요.

기출 문제 안에서 있었던 것들은 다 무난하게 답했고 그렇지 않았던 문제들도 일 경험 토대로 답변 준비한 것들을 생각하면서 풀어나갔습니다. 계속 적극적으로 미소를 잃지 않고 말했고, 면접이 끝나고 문을 열고 나오는 순간까지도 워킹, 미소 다 생각하면서 걸었습니다.

그리고 3월 20일! ACZ링크를 받았습니다.

2018년 카타르 부산 채용 후기2

CV DROP (First day)

저는 오후 4시로 받아서 천천히 부산으로 내려갔습니다. CV drop은 더욱이 다른 스테이지 보다 짧은 시간 안에 끝나기 때문에 전체적으로 보여주는 이미지가 좋아야 해서 화장을 카타르 이미지에 맞게 고치고 또 고치고 세심하게 신경썼어요!

저는 문밖에서부터 미소장착을 하면서 기다렸어요. 제 차례가 되었을땐, 힘차고 당당한 걸음으로 웃으며 면접관께 다가갔고 물론! 먼저 인사를 건넸어요! 저한테는 두 가지 질문을 하셨습니다.

1. What do think about adopting a child?

2. What do you think the customer expectation is?

저는 긍정적이게 대답을 하고 바로 암리치를 쟀습니다. 암리치를 재러 걸어갈때도 면접관이 항상 보고 있다는 말을 기억하며! 차분히 끝냈고 돌아보니 면접관님께서 인비를 이미 적고 계셨습니다.

Assessment day (Second day)

이번 채용에 지원자가 상당히 많은 관계로 저는 CV Drop 바로 다음날 어쎄스데이를 하지 않고 그 다음날 오게 되었습니다.

적어도 30분 전에는 도착해서 옆 지원자들과 친해지고, 제 시간에 맞춰 면접관님들이 들어오셨습니다. 카타르 프레젠테이션을 하는 도중에도 계속 미소를 띄우고 있었고 바로 영어테스트를 했습니다. 저희 조는 모두가 영어테스트 통과했습니다! 그후, 1-70번 (아니타 마리아), 70-142번 (아가 티나) 두 조로 나뉘어서 암리치, 스카첵, 스몰톡을 진행하였습니다. 들어가자마자 먼저 인사하고 바로 암리치 재고 (신발 벗을 때도 조심히 … 저는 신발 한 쪽이 쓰러져서 가지런히 다시 놓았답니다! 이런 자세도 다 본답니다.) 질문은 또 2가지 받았습니다.

1. Any food you can cook? What are the two ingredients that is important for that food?

2. What do you think about the customer expectation?

Cv drop 때랑 면접관이 달라졌는데 똑같은 질문을 우연히 또 받았답니다.

Final interview (Second day)

럭키하게도! 어쎄스 스테이지에서 통과된 사람들은 전부다 파이널로!!!! 퍼블릭 스피킹과 그림묘사는 생략되었습니다. 반이상의 지원자들이 떨어지고, 오후 팀이 없는 관계로 아가 티나 조의 16명 정도의 지원자들은 바로 파이널을 봤습니다. 하루종일 이루어진 면접이지만 저희보다는 면접관님들이 더 힘들다는걸 명심하고 활기차게 들어갔어요. 밝게 먼저 인사하는걸 절대 빼먹지 않았죠! 한 면접관께서 질문을 하고 다른 면접관께서 옆에서 적었는데 한분의 익숙치 않은 발음 때문에 질문 몇개는 다시 물어봐야 했었어요. 대답을 하면서 질문을 한 면접관만 보고 이야기하는게 아니라, 면접관 두 분께 아이컨택을 하나하나 했습니다. 대답을 할땐, 항상 웃으며 천천히. 끝이 나고 나올 때도 제 뒷모습을 보고 있다고 생각하고 끝까지 가지런히 하면서 나왔습니다!

2019년 카타르 부산 채용 후기1

CV Drop

저는 티나에게 인비를 받았고, 사실 티나를 유럽 오픈에서 한번 본 적이 있어서 제가 적극적으로 먼저 인사하고 다가갔습니다.

제가 받은 질문은 오픈데이에서 자기 어디서 봤는지?, 그때 어느 스테이지에서 떨어졌는지?, 그때 센텐스 슈팅 뭐였어?, 지금 네가 생각하는 그 센텐스 슈팅 답은?, Yonng People이 overrated된다 생각해? 이렇게 였고 저는 티나 그루밍 칭찬하면서 친근하게 다가가니 티나가 정말 좋아하면서 인비 써주었어요.

제가 생각하는 CV의 핵심은 밝은 미소와 차분하게 면접관 포스에 눌려 말 흐리지 말고 하고 싶은 말 끝까지 다 하는 거에요!

영어테스트

영어테스트는 정말 쉬워요! 지문 읽고 그대로 풀면 됩니다. 계산문제는 없어졌고 동의어 찾는 문제 끝에 나와요. 여기서 오후 어세스 총 150명 중 10명 정도 떨어지신 것 같아요.

암리치, 스카첵, 스몰톡

공포의 스카첵 단계지요. 가장 뚫기 힘든 단계이고 제가 이 단계에서 다수 떨어져봐서 고민을 많이 했었습니다. 저는 아니타 마리아 조였고, 늦은 밤까지 진행되어 면접관이 굉장히 지쳐 있는 상태였습니다. 저는 "이럴수록 더 밝고 에너지 있게 다가가서 면접관 혼을 빼놓자"라고 다짐했고 지치지만 절대 지친 티 내지 않고 더 적극적으로 다가갔습니다. 들어가자마자 큰소리로 Good evening, 면접관 이름 부르며 각각 아이컨택 했습니다. 암리치 먼저 하고 오라고 해서 신발 가지런히 벗고 암리치했고 자리에 앉으면서 면접관에게 다시 만나 반갑다고(이전 오픈데이에서 만난적 있음), 너무 만나고 싶었다고 적극적으로 웃으면서 다가갔던 것이, 지쳤던 면접관에게 다른 지원자들과

조금 다른 모습으로 제가 비춰졌던 것 같습니다.

스카첵에서 제가 생각하는 핵심은 혹시 스카가 있다면, 스카 말할 때도 당당하게, 한마디라도 더 붙여서 자신을 어필하는 것이라 생각합니다.

제가 받은 질문으로는 한국 블로그 문화, 지난 오픈데이 이후로 무엇이 발전했는지, 너 시크릿 펄슨이야?, 고객이 서비스에 큰 기대 갖는거 어떻게 생각해? 등등 제가 하는 답변마다 다 꼬리 질문 있었지만, 제가 일전에 떨어졌을 때와 차이점은 정말 커뮤니케이션이 잘 이루어진다는 느낌을 받았습니다. 약간 동네 언니들과 이야기하는 느낌이랄까요? 면접관 두 분이 제 발음 교정도 해주셨는데 저는 직접 팔로잉 하면서, 배우며 잘 따르는 모습 보여드렸습니다. 나가기 전엔 인사드리며 꼭 도하에서 볼 수 있었으면 좋겠다고, 다른 오픈데이 도시가 아니라! 이렇게 말하니 면접관이 웃으면서 메이비 넥스트 스테이지? 하길래 감사하다고 하면서 나왔습니다.

운이 좋게도 밤 늦은 시각까지 딜레이가 되는 바람에 퍼블릭 스피치는 생략하고 바로 파이널 리스트 발표가 났으며 바로 파이널폼 작성했습니다. 저는 여느 오픈데이 어세스먼트에서 항상 자리에 앉아 있을 때의 팁을 말씀 드리자면 맨 앞자리에 앉아서 면접관 눈에 잘 띄려고 노력했어요. 진짜 보면 앞에 있을 때 성적이 좀 좋았던 것 같아요. 자세 꼿꼿하게 유지하려고 노력했고 바로 앞에 면접관 있으니 너무 면접관 쳐다보지 않고 앞의 허공을 바라보며 미소를 계속 유지했습니다.

대망의 파이널

면접장에서 드디어 제 차례가 되어 아니타 마리아를 다시 만났고 힘차게 인사했습니다. 면접관과 파이널폼 체크하며 제가 채우지 못한 부분 같이 확인하며 체크했습니다. 면접관이 도와주면 무조건 땡큐 땡큐 하면서 인사 하는거 잊지 않았구요. 제가 제 2외국어 스페인어 할 줄 안다고 적어놓으니 마리아가 스페인어로 물어보더라구요. 바로 스페인어 두어 문장이어도 뻔뻔하게 당황하지 않고 답변했고 잘한다고 칭찬해주시니 저도 '그라시아쓰' 하면서 더 웃으면서 다가갔습니다.

제가 받은 질문은 Yes or No 질문들!(머리염색 했는지, 젤네일인지, 교정 했는지, 알콜서브, 변화 어떻게 생각하는지, 위닝팀 경험 등등 약 15개 넘는 질문) 면접관이 먼저 농담해주면서 전반적으로 친근한 분위기였습니다.

저자소개_ 이 혜 진

학력 및 경력

- 한양대학교 일반대학원 관광학 박사수료
- 한양대학교 국제관광대학원 국제관광학 석사
- 한국형 에니어그램 강사:해석상담사
- 채용면접전문가 1급
- 심리상담사 1급
- 영어회화능력검정사 1급
- 퍼스널컬러컨설턴트 1급
- 와인소믈리에 1급
- Emirates Aviation College : Leadership training course 수료(Managing Business, Inspired People, Managing Passenger, Professional Image, Managing Crew, Professional Knowledge, Managing Resource 과정 수료)

현) 오산대학교 항공서비스과 교수

전) 세한대학교 항공서비스학과 교수
　　두원공과대학교 항공서비스과 겸임교수
　　항공,호텔,관광 관련학과 다수 대학교 출강
　　외국항공사 객실승무원 및 지상직 1차 대표 면접관
　　(에미레이트항공, 카타르항공, 말레이시아항공,
　　필리핀항공,퍼시픽항공 외 다수)
　　KLM네덜란드항공 객실승무원(비지니스 클래스),
　　한국인 기내통역관
　　에미레이트항공 일등석 선임승무원, B/C부사무장
　　KOTRA (두바이 본부) 영어통역 다수
　　한국관광공사 (두바이 본부) VIP 관광통역 다수
　　파라다이스 워커힐호텔 외국인전용 카지노딜러

외항사 면접관이 알려주는
단기 합격을 위한 완벽 가이드

항공 영어 인터뷰

초판 1쇄 발행　2016년　3월 10일
3판 1쇄 발행　2024년　8월　5일

저　자　　이 혜 진
펴낸이　　임 순 재
펴낸곳　　**(주)한올출판사**
등　록　　제11-403호
주　소　　서울시 마포구 모래내로 83(성산동 한올빌딩 3층)
전　화　　(02) 376-4298(대표)
팩　스　　(02) 302-8073
홈페이지　www.hanol.co.kr
e-메일　　hanol@hanol.co.kr
ISBN　　979-11-6647-468-2

항공 영어 인터뷰